THE PILGRIM LIBRARY OF WORLD RELIGIONS

EVIL AND SUFFERING

EDITED BY JACOB NEUSNER

⅁LWR

The Pilgrim Press
Cleveland, Ohio

The Pilgrim Press, Cleveland, Ohio
© 1998 by Jacob Neusner

03   02   01   00   99   98   5   4   3   2   1

Library of Congress Cataloging-in-Publication Data

Evil and suffering / edited by Jacob Neusner.
     p.   cm. — (The Pilgrim library of world religions)
     Includes bibliographical references.
     ISBN 0-8298-1249-0 (paper : alk. paper)
     1. Good and evil—Comparative studies.   2. Suffering—Religious
aspects—Comparative studies.   I. Neusner, Jacob, 1932–   .
II. Series.
BJ1406.E95   1998
291.2'118—dc21   98-36235
                                                     CIP

CONTENTS

The great world religions address certain existential issues in common, for the human situation raises compelling questions that transcend the limits of time, space, and circumstance. Recognizing that each religion forms a system with its own definitive traits, we aver that all religions must and do treat in common a range of fundamental topics. We hold that comparison and contrast among religions begins with the treatment of urgent questions that all of them must address and somehow resolve. This library introduces the religions of the world as they meet in conversation on the profound issues of world order—transcendent, individual and familial, and social. In the first rubric falls how we know God; in the second, our life of suffering and death, women, and the aspiration for afterlife; and in the third, the authority and continuity of tradition itself. Indeed, for the purpose of these volumes we may define religion as a theory of the social order that addresses from the unique perspective of transcendence (some prefer "the sacred," others, "God," in concrete language) issues of the human condition of home and family on the one side, and of the public interest on the other.

The five topics of the initial account require only brief clarification. Common to the human condition is the quest for God. Everyone suffers and everyone dies. One-half of humanity is comprised of women. Humanity everywhere aspires to explain what happens after we die. And, finally, every religion identifies authoritative teaching ("sacred texts"), though what the various religions mean by "a text" will vary, since a person or a drama or a dance as much as a piece of writing may form a fixed and official statement for amplification and exegesis through time. In these five volumes, the initial set in the Pilgrim Library of World Religions, we take up the five topics we deem both critical and ubiquitous in the religions we identify as paramount. Following a single outline, worked out in common, we spell out how each religion addresses the topic at hand. In this way we propose to make possible a labor of comparison of religions: how all address a single issue, uniformly defined. We represent the statement of each religion within that common pattern, so that where the world religions concur and where they diverge becomes apparent.

The religions are chosen because all of them not only speak to humanity in common but also relate to one another in concrete, historical ways. Judaism, Christianity, and Islam join together in a common doctrine of the unity of God and in valuing a common scripture—the Hebrew Scriptures of ancient Israel. Judaism knows these Scriptures as the written Torah, which is the Old Testament of Christianity. In the case of Christianity and Islam, the Old and New Testaments are joined into the Bible, "the Book." Hinduism forms the matrix out of which Buddhism took shape, much as the ancient Israelite scriptures, amplified by the Judaism of the day, defined the matrix in which Christianity originated. Not only do Judaism, Christianity, and Islam conduct an ongoing dialogue between and among themselves, but Christianity and Islam compete in Africa, and Hinduism and Islam in India. All five religions not only address humanity but reach across the boundaries of ethnic groups and local societies and speak of the condition of humanity. And all five come to formulation in a set of writings deemed classical and authoritative.

That fact—that each of the religions treated here identifies a canon that defines the faith—makes the work of this series possible. For each of the religions treated here proves diverse; viewed over time, all of them show marks of historical change and diversity of doctrine and practice alike. Take Judaism, for example. Today it comprises a number of distinct religious systems, or Judaisms—for example, Reform, Orthodox, and Conservative in North America. Christianity has three vast divisions: Catholic, Protestant, and Orthodox. The world has gotten to know some of the differences between Shi'ite and Sunni Islam. The upshot is that while we recognize the density and diversity of each of the religions under study in these volumes, our account of their principal doctrines on critical and universal issues appeals only to those writings that all forms or versions of the several religions acknowledge, to which all Judaisms or all Christianities, for instance, will appeal.

That same fact—the appeal to authoritative writings of a classical character—also permits us to describe without nuance of context or historical circumstance the positions of the five religions. People who practice the religions set forth here may believe diverse things within the respective frameworks of those religions; Catholics may practice birth control, for example. So too, religions that bear a distinctive relationship to a given ethnic group—Judaism to Jews, for instance—cannot be defined merely by public-opinion polling of that ethnic group. Not all Jews practice Judaism; not all Arabs, Islam; and not all Italians, Catholicism. By concentrating on the classical statements of the religions at hand, we set forth an ideal type, the picture of the religion that its authoritative writings provide, not the picture of the religion that the workaday world may yield.

The same consideration affects the diversity over time and in contemporary life of the several religions before us. Everyone understands that all five religions not only produced diverse systems, but also developed and changed over history, so that a doctrine or belief on a given topic in one time and place may not conform to the shape of the same doctrine or belief on the same topic in a different setting. Ideas about God vary, for instance, depending on the situation of the interpreter—learned, or mystic, or simple, for instance—or on the age in which the idea is explained. That is quite natural, given the vast stretches of time and space traversed by the five religions we examine.

While acknowledging the variations produced by the passage of time and the movement of culture, we appeal to the classical writings for an account that all later generations of the faithful, wherever located, can affirm, however diverse the interpretations placed on that account. In the appendix, Literary Sources of the World Religions, each of the writers lists the documents that form the foundation of his chapter in this volume.

To begin with, this library took shape in the shared intellectual adventure that joins some of us together as professors of the academic study of religion at Bard College and in dialogue with our students there. We tried out the various chapters on them. The chapters were outlined in common.

All of us express our appreciation to the president of Bard College, Dr. Leon Botstein, and Dean of Faculty Stuart Levine for their encouragement of this project; and to Mr. Timothy G. Staveteig and Ms. Marjorie Pon of The Pilgrim Press, whose good ideas always made the work still more challenging and stimulating than our joint venture had made it to begin with.

CONTRIBUTORS

JONATHAN BROCKOPP received his Ph.D. from Yale University. He is assistant professor of religion at Bard College.

BRUCE CHILTON is chairman of the Department of Religion, Bernard Iddings Bell Professor of Religion, and chaplain of Bard College.

CHARLES HALLISEY is John L. Loeb Associate Professor of the Humanities, Harvard University.

JACOB NEUSNER is distinguished research professor of religious studies at the University of South Florida and professor of religion at Bard College.

BRIAN K. SMITH is professor of religious studies at the University of California, Riverside.

PUBLISHER'S NOTE

The Pilgrim Press is a leading publisher in Christian ethics and theology. Through the Pilgrim Library of World Religions series, edited by Jacob Neusner, we seek to continue and expand this heritage.

Part of this heritage is a policy regarding the use of inclusive language for human beings and for God. With few exceptions, the Pilgrim Library of World Religions maintains this policy. Nevertheless we recognize that various religious traditions have struggled differently with inclusive language for God. Therefore each contributor, especially when discussing God's self-revelation, has been offered some flexibility in order to faithfully reflect that religious tradition's current form of expression.

When we come to the question of evil and suffering, we find that the three monotheist religions, Judaism, Christianity, and Islam, radically differ from the two polytheist religions, Hinduism and Buddhism, considered in these pages. For to begin with, evil and suffering represent obstacles to faith and understanding only for those who believe God is unique and all-powerful and also benevolent. The faithful will wonder why bad things happen to good people, and, conversely, since God is just, why good things happen to bad people.

A religion of numerous gods finds many solutions to one problem; a religion of only one God answers many problems with one solution. Life is seldom fair. Rules rarely work. To explain the reason why, polytheisms adduce multiple causes of chaos, a god per anomaly: Diverse gods do various things, so, it stands to reason, outcomes ordinarily conflict. Monotheism by nature explains many things in a single way: One God rules; life is meant to be fair, and just rules are supposed to describe what is ordinary, all in the name of that one and only God. So in monotheism a simple logic governs to limit ways of making sense of things. But that logic contains its own dialectics. If one true God has done everything, then, since this God is all-powerful and omniscient, all things are credited to, and blamed on, God. This God can be either good or bad, just or unjust—but not both. Within the logic of monotheism, one may frame in only a few ways the problem of evil and suffering.

Hinduism, for its part, finds it possible to see evil and suffering as "necessary to, and part of the balance of, the cosmos as a whole. But beyond and behind this phenomenal world is true reality, where evil and suffering do not exist." So states Brian K. Smith in his chapter. But for Christianity, Judaism, and Islam, evil and suffering not only do exist, but they represent the result of willful activity, whether evil is personified as Satan, an active force and opposite of God, or whether suffering is represented as God's punishment of individuals' sinfulness. So too, the Buddhist approach, which differentiates among types of suffering, begins with the view of suffering caused "by the fact of just being born." The other classes—illness, physical discomfort, mental and emotional distress—contrast with the monotheist religions' homogenization of all evil and suffering into a single, massive dilemma. As Charles Hallisey frames the matter, "Suffering is a problem in and of itself, something no one wants and no one seeks." But in Buddhism it is difficult to find a counterpart to the monotheist religions' view that suffering is not a problem to be solved but a challenge to faith. As he says, "Suffering is caused by desire, and we will be able to stop suffering in a permanent way only when we are able to stop desire." Contrast the view of the monotheisms that suffering represents a punishment caused by our own conduct, the compensation for rebellion against God, something that God inflicts upon us!

When we come to Christianity, Judaism, and Islam, we find ourselves in a different world altogether. Now the givenness of suffering meets its challenge. The three monotheist religions concur on the basic principle that suffering and evil represent flaws in creation and problems to be addressed. But each finds its own points of stress, and to regard the position of all three as essentially the same would be an error.

As Bruce Chilton frames Christianity's position, "The fact of our human mortality carries innumerable forms of suffering and pain with it, and that would seem to make it extremely difficult to understand how God, as a loving and merciful father, can have created a world so riven with evil." Suffering then stands for evil; it is not a given to be accepted but embodies a crisis of faith in God's character. Orthodox Christianity affirmed, and heretical, Gnostic Christianity denied, the goodness of God as known in the world. Both agreed, then, that evil is caused, not just a given, and that evil presents a question to be answered, not just a reality to be adjusted to. Before the confrontation of the two Christianities of the second century, the Orthodox and the Gnostic, concerning the character of God—known and good, or known and evil, unknown and redemptive—a prior question had to be settled. That question concerned the anomalous character of the wickedness in the world—indeed, of the very character of the world. No wonder, then, that in Christianity, as in Judaism and Islam, evil could be conceived as "the devil" or "Satan," a being that actually exists in competition with God.

In Judaism too, when confronted with the problem of evil, the faithful turn first to their own sin as the explanation. Defined in the model of the first sin, the one committed by human beings in Eden, sin is an act of rebellion against God. Rebellion takes two forms. As a gesture of omission, sin embodies the failure to carry out one's obligation to God set forth in the Torah. As one of commission, it constitutes an act of defiance. In both cases sin comes about through our intentionality to reject the will of God, set forth in the Torah. However accomplished, whether through omission or commission, an act becomes sinful because of the attitude that accompanies it. That is why human beings are responsible for sin, and hence cause their own suffering, answerable to God in particular, who may be said to take the matter personally, just as it is meant. The consequence of sin is death for the individual, exile and estrangement for holy Israel, and disruption for the world. That is why sin accounts for much of the flaw of creation. What is at stake in sin is succinctly stated: it accounts for the deplorable condition of the world, defined by the situation of Israel. But sin is not a permanent feature of world order. It is a detail of an orderly progression, as God to begin with had planned, from chaos, which gave way to creation, to the Torah, which after the Flood through Israel restored order to the world, and onward to the age of perfection.

Thus we are able to outline the context in which evil and

suffering find their importance. Judaism's sages never for one minute doubted that the world order of justice encompassed private lives. This they stated in countless ways, the simplest being the representation of Hillel's statement encased in a fragmentary narrative: One day he was walking along the river and he saw a skull floating on the water and said to it, "Because you drowned others, they drowned you, and in the end those who drowned you will be drowned." Somewhere, somehow, the wicked get their comeuppance. The just God sees to it. But what about the righteous? Is their just reward equally certain? However dubious the former of the two propositions—the ultimate triumph of justice over the wicked when a crime or sin has been committed—that the righteous get their just reward certainly conflicted, then as now, with everyday experience. Indeed, the basic conviction of world order defined by justice violated every intuition, every perception, every reflection upon humanity's fate that private lives provoked. Then as now people lived in a world of caprice and, right or wrong, discerned no justice at all. But suffering on its own constitutes a form of expiation and atonement, no less than an offering in the Temple in olden times. Second, suffering alerts us to our having sinned, telling us to find out what sin we have done and to repent for that sin. The prophets said the same thing to all Israel that the sages say to Israelites. This kind of suffering represents an act of benevolence as well and is to be desired; it requires no justification beyond its own purpose. While we deal with the classical statements of the several religions studied in these pages, we cannot miss the urgency brought to the question of suffering and evil by the Holocaust.

Islam concurs in its fundamental logic with Judaism and Christianity: suffering bears rational causes, whether of one's own or others' doing. Islam affirms the world as an essentially good place, as Jonathan Brockopp insists. Suffering comes about because people step outside the path that God has laid out. Pain is not always suffering, and suffering is not always evil. Suffering may represent God's way of alleviating greater suffering, but God does not will evil upon humanity. We may not always recognize God's goodness, but God is always good and just. Above all, evil results from human action. And the greatest cause of evil is human action, perhaps the action of others. How should we respond to evil and suffering? By staying on God's path of right action. We have the power, Islam maintains, to confront evil by recognizing it for what it is. Humanity can save itself from perdition: "the real problem lies within man himself, for he is a blend of good and evil, ignorance and knowledge, power and impotence." Our power to distinguish right from wrong allows us to see Satan's footsteps. Muslims see the world as basically good, the perfect creation of God. That is the starting point for Islamic, as much as for Judaic and Christian, thinking about evil and suffering. In this way, Islam concurs with Judaism and Christianity that humanity bears the burden of its own condition, which is not natural and not given but anomalous and self-inflicted.

No topic taken up in this series so engages the faithful of religions West and East, because when we speak of suffering and evil, we address the human condition. When we address in detail how the five great religions treated here formulate matters, we do well to concentrate, first of all, on how the doctrines of evil and suffering fit into the larger religious systems of world construction constituted by those religions. For no detail, however critical, stands on its own. What a religion says about one topic, it says about all topics, and each detail in a well-crafted structure bears the weight and message of the whole structure. Our task is not to decide whether we agree with the several theories of evil and suffering reviewed in these pages, but how we understand and make sense of them in each respective religious context. The precipitating question for class discussion is: Why does this religion find this framing of matters rational? What larger rationality encompasses this account of the human condition?

But if the academic framework in which we study comparative religion aims to increase understanding, still, we also, many of us, engage in the study of religion because we are, each in his or her way and social context, parties to religion. We study the subject because we care about it. And in that context, questions of plausibility, even judgments of truth, demand a hearing. Take the obvious case of Judaism, for example, with its acute contemporary engagement with the Holocaust. What words can possibly frame the question of the Holocaust in such a way that the doctrines of the Torah (that is, Judaism viewed whole) constitute a compelling response? That issue, at the cutting edge of the religious life today, finds its counterparts in Islam and Christianity. And take the claim of Buddhism and Hinduism that we can stop suffering when we stop wanting. Does such a reading of the human condition resolve the issue in all its dimensions? So too at some point we have to ask ourselves whether we find plausible the allegations of Islam and Buddhism and Christianity and Hinduism and Judaism—or the secular position that holds suffering to bear no meaning whatever—whether we find compelling any of these positions at all. So these essays mean to provoke private thought and public debate about how we should regard evil and suffering and respond to the condition of humanity and of the world—and the character of God as well.

In the pages of this book we mean to provide systematic and informed accounts of how the five religions deal with the question at hand, and we believe we have done so. But we maintain that religions that claim to speak truth, not just form cultural systems of belief and behavior, should be taken at their word—and judged by those to whom they speak and also by those to whom they do not speak.

CHAPTER I

Hinduism

WHY ARE EVIL, SUFFERING, AND PAIN A PROBLEM FOR HINDUISM?

The problem of "evil" (however this concept is defined) and suffering (physical, emotional, psychological, existential, or spiritual pain and malaise) is usually seen as one of the universals in the study of religion. All religions, it can be said, have ideas and terms that correlate to notions of evil and suffering; and all religions, albeit in varying ways, have struggled with the problems surrounding the existence of evil and proffered ways to alleviate human suffering.

Different religions, however, understand these terms differently and present differing solutions to the problems they pose. Furthermore, religions are not—despite the claims to the contrary often put forward by their adherents, theologians, and philosophers—monolithic entities. Within any religion there will be different traditions, sects, and intellectual schools, each with its own—and often radically different—approach to the problems of (and solutions to) evil and suffering.

One major divide on this question is between religious traditions that embrace the doctrine of monotheism, those that are theistic but envision the divine in dualistic or pluralistic terms, and those that conceive of the powers that govern evil and suffering in the world in nontheistic terms. For monotheistic traditions in which God is understood to be both omnipotent and benevolent, the existence of evil and suffering poses major philosophical difficulties. It is in these contexts that the classic form of theodicy can be found. The paradox is aptly summed up by the modern philosopher of religion John Hick: "If God is perfectly good, He must want to abolish all evil; if He is unlimitedly powerful, He must be able to abolish all evil; but evil exists; therefore either God is not perfectly good or He is not unlimitedly powerful."[1] Theistic traditions that portray the divine in dualistic or pluralistic forms can circumvent this quandary to some extent by introducing competing demonic forces (e.g., a devil or demons) who are held responsible for the introduction and perpetuation of evil and suffering among human beings. Finally, there are traditions in which evil and suffering are not attributed either to a benevolent and omnipotent God or to superhuman demonic powers, but rather to human beings themselves or, simply, to the very constitution and automatic workings of the universe.

Hinduism, being an extremely variegated and complex set of traditions with many different strands, has within it versions of all these positions, with their varying ideas of the origins and dilemmas of evil and suffering. Hinduism thus can be compared to other religions (and to other traditions within other religions); at the same time its unique formulations, history, and cultural contextualization must also be recognized.

One way that the four-thousand-year-old and multifarious entity we call Hinduism has been analyzed is into three principal types of religious traditions: those that stress works or "action" (*karma*), those that center on wisdom or efficacious religious knowledge (*jnana*), and those that emphasize devotionalism to a personalized God (*bhakti*). Each of these types of traditions has understood the problem of evil and suffering somewhat differently (although overlaps and agreements also exist), and each has offered distinct "solutions" to the problems entailed and distinctive methods for overcoming evil and suffering and obtaining salvation. "Evil" is, no matter how it is understood, a relative term; it is, minimally, the "absence or opposite of good." Different conceptualizations of evil and suffering will include varying representations of "the Good" and how to attain it.

HOW IS SUFFERING REPRESENTED AND PERCEIVED AND EXPERIENCED?

The Vedic period provides us with the earliest form of religion in India emphasizing action or works. Vedism revolved entirely around the performance and ideology of the sacrifice, an extremely intricate and complex ritual centering on the offering into fire of oblations dedicated to one or another of the many gods of the pantheon. The original meaning of the term karma is "ritual action," that is, correctly and precisely executed activity that will have a salutary effect on the participants of the ritual and, indeed, on the universe as a whole. Karma in this sense was the antidote to "evil" and suffering. Among the principal connotations of various terms that might be translated as "evil" in this period are those that refer to the imperfections inherent in the world of nature.

The philosophy underlying Vedic ritualism assumed that the universe was, in the beginning, created by a god (Purusa, the Cosmic Man, or Prajapati, the "Lord of Creatures"), but that this work was defective. The creator "emits" from himself the creation, but in this cosmogonic move from primordial unity to multiplicity and diversity, the cosmogonic product is characterized by disconnection, confusion, and disarray. The parts of time, too, are created disconnected and "disjointed": "When Prajapati had emitted the creatures, his joints became disjointed. Now Prajapati is the year, and his joints are the two junctures of day and night, of the waxing and waning lunar half-months, and of the beginnings of the seasons. He was unable to rise with his joints disjointed" (Satapatha Brahmana 1.6.3. 35).

The point of such Vedic myths of origins is to represent God's cosmogonic activity as faulty; creation here is not cosmos. The universe, as it was in the beginning, is in need of repair. And it is precisely the ritual activity (both of the gods and of human beings) that is designed to "fix" the universe. "Evil," here in the sense of chaos, is overcome by the restorative, connective powers of action, of karma.

The Vedic sacrifice was performed to continually "heal" a world that was created faulty and perpetually tends toward its "natural" state of chaos. The ritual was conceived as a connective, reparative activity. "With the Agnihotra [the twice-daily sacrifice performed at dawn and dusk] they healed that joint [which is] the two junctures of night and day, and joined it together. With the new and full moon sacrifices, they healed that joint [which is] between the waxing and waning lunar half-months, and joined it together. And with the Caturmasyas [performed quarterly at the beginning of the seasons] they healed that joint [which is] the beginning of the seasons, and joined it together" (Satapatha Brahmana 1.6.3.36).

Not only was ritual action supposed to have such cosmological powers, but it was also the means by which a person, born also in the natural state of defectiveness, was constructed into a proper human being. Rituals beginning with the *samskaras*—rites of passage performed at critical junctures in the life of a youth—had as their purpose to repair the imperfections of birth. Among these life-cycle rites, the most important was the *upanayana,* a rite of initiation into the study of the Veda and performance of sacrifice. It is regarded as a "second birth," a birth "out of the Veda" or "out of the sacrifice." While Vedic fire sacrifices tended to be eclipsed by other forms of religious practice in later Hinduism, the performance of the samskaras has continued to the present day and is done for much the same reason.

The more complex sacrifices of the Vedic ritual repertoire

were supposed to have a constructive effect on the identity of the sacrificer and were also designed to help overcome the problems faced in this life and, potentially, in the next. "Man is born into a world made by himself" through the rituals he performs, declares one text (Satapatha Brahmana 6.2.2.7); one's identity or stature in this world was the product of the sacrifices one offers. Sacrifice was the means to overcome various forms of evil and suffering in this life. In Vedic times, "evil" could mean any number of afflictions that stood in the way of a good life: poor crops, hunger, illness, loss in battle, poverty, the absence of sons, constriction of one's freedom and sphere of influence, and also ritual error (which was supposed to have disastrous consequences).

It could also, of course, mean death. Ritual activity, it was often said, was the means to escape death: "Born out of the sacrifice, the sacrificer frees himself from death. The sacrifice becomes his self" (Satapatha Brahmana 1.3.2.1). Being "free from death" in this period could simply refer to living a long life; "immortality" sometimes is defined as living to the age of one hundred. But it could also mean a rebirth after death in "heaven" or the "world of the gods," a place in the afterlife that is also tied to one's karma or ritual activity during life on earth. Conversely, those who do not perform sacrifices, who revile the Brahmin priests, or who commit other "sins" are relegated to various hells, the horrors of which are vividly depicted.

The notion that one's own *ritual* acts (for in Vedic times, these were the only ones that really mattered) had consequences (in the future as well as the present) is one of the possible sources for a post-Vedic doctrine that was to have huge implications for the religious worldview of all subsequent Indian traditions. This was the doctrine that stated that *all* actions produced fruit, good or bad, that determined the quality of one's life. This causal and moral "law of karma" first appears in Hindu texts dating to the middle of the first millennium B.C.E.

and also features as a prominent doctrine in the new religions that arose in India at this time, Buddhism and Jainism.

In its earliest appearances, this doctrine of rebirth after death is regarded as a "secret" doctrine, to be revealed by a teacher only to a well-prepared student. Furthermore, the source of karma is located in desire, which begins a causal chain—from desire comes resolve, from resolve comes action, and from action comes karmic reaction:

> "Yajnavalkya," said [Artabhaga, the student], "when the voice of a dead man goes into fire, his breath into wind, his eye into the sun, his mind into the moon, his hearing into the quarters of heaven, his body into the earth, his soul into space, the hairs of his head into plants, the hairs of his body into trees, and his blood and semen are placed in water, what then becomes of this person?" "Artabhaga, my dear, take my hand. We two only will know of this. This is not for us two [to speak of] in public." The two went away and deliberated. What they said was karma. What they praised was karma. Verily, one becomes good by good action, bad by bad action. . . . According as one acts, according as one conducts himself, so does he become. The doer of good becomes good. The doer of evil becomes evil. One becomes virtuous by virtuous action, bad by bad action. But people say: "A person is made [not of acts, but] of desires only." [In reply to this I say:] As is his desire, such is his resolve; as is his resolve, such the action he performs; what action [karma] he performs, that he procures for himself.[2]

This new concept of a "law of karma"—whereby good acts result in good results, bad in bad—extends the Vedic notion of consequential action from the confines of the ritual to the whole of life. It also expands the notion of humans' responsibility for their fate from the ritual sphere (where, in the Vedic period, one counters evil and suffering by acts that construct a better self and "world" for the sacrificer in this life and the next) to life as a whole. Thus, from this point on in Hinduism, human beings can be held responsible for *both* the good and the evil elements of their lives: one reaps what one sows, and such moral causality operates in the universe as an automatic "law."

The law of karma also presupposes a series of past and future lives. Deeds done in past lives determine the circumstances of one's present existence, and one never knows when the fruits of those actions will ripen: "The acts done in former births never abandon any creature. . . . [And] since man lives under the control of karma, he must always be alert to ways of maintaining his equilibrium and of avoiding evil consequences" (*Mahabharata* 3.207.19–20). This theory also assumes future lives, not just in heavens or hells but in this world or any of a potentially infinite number of world systems. Finally, it presupposes that one may be reborn in any of these locales as any number of entities, ranging from gods to inanimate objects; good karma obviously would entail a better rebirth, and bad karma results in a worse existence.

Karma is the by-product of activity, but Hindu texts often analyze the sources of karma quite thoroughly. We have seen that desire (in general, of all sorts) is pinpointed as one such origin. The sources of karma are enumerated in the following text as three—originating in the "mind-and-heart," in speech, and in the body—and each type produces distinctive consequences and future rebirths:

> The action [karma] that arises in the mind-and-heart, speech, and the body bears good and bad fruits; the highest, lowest, and middle levels of men's existences come from their actions. Know that the mind-and-heart sets in motion the body's [action] here on earth, which is of three kinds and has three bases and ten distinctive marks. The three kinds of [bad] mental action are thinking too much about things that belong to others, meditating in

one's mind-and-heart about what is undesirable, and adhering to falsehoods. The four kinds of [bad] speech [acts] are verbal abuse, lies, slander of all sorts, and unbridled chatter. The three kinds of [bad] bodily [action] are traditionally said to be taking things that have not been given, committing violence against the law, and having sex with another man's wife. A man experiences in his mind-and-heart the good or bad effects of past actions committed in his mind-and-heart, in his speech what he has committed in his speech, and in his body what he has committed with his body. A man becomes a stationary object as a result of the faults that are the effects of past [bad] actions of the body, a bird or wild animal from those of speech, and a member of one of the lowest castes from those of the mind-and-heart.[3]

Another text posits an exact, and sometimes amusing, correlation between evil deeds and the consequences visited upon the evildoer subsequently. The passage begins by noting that "Some evil-hearted men undergo a reverse transformation of their form because of evil practices here [in this life], and some because of those committed in a former life."

A man who steals gold has mangled fingernails; a man who drinks liquor has discoloured teeth; a priest-killer suffers from consumption; and a man who violates his guru's marriage-bed has a diseased skin. A slanderer has a putrid nose; an informer, a putrid mouth; a man who steals grain lacks a part of his body, but an adulterator of grain has a superfluity [of parts of his body]. A thief of food has indigestion; a thief of words is a mute; a man who steals clothing has white leprosy; and a horse-thief is lame. A man who steals lamps becomes blind, and a man who extinguishes lamps, one-eyed; a sadist is always sick, and an adulterer is rheumatic. Thus, because of the particular effects of their past actions, men who are despised by good people are born idiotic, mute, blind, deaf, and deformed.

—Manusmrti 11.48–54

The theory of transmigration of souls was introduced into Indian religions more or less simultaneously with the notion that the cycle of perpetual birth, death, and rebirth occurs not just at the level of human beings but is descriptive of the universe as a whole. The Sanskrit name for this theory is *samsara*, a word that literally means "to wander or pass through a series of states or conditions." Samsara describes the beginningless and endless cycle of cosmic or universal death and rebirth; all of phenomenal existence is thought to be transient, ever changing, and cyclical. In somewhat later times, the cycle is said to involve the fall from a Golden Age of happiness and righteousness. Increasingly degenerative cosmic eras occur until the universe passes into the present evil age, the Kali Yuga, at the end of which the cycle begins again.

The term *samsara* describes this conditioned, ever changing, and cyclical phenomenal universe in which souls, fueled by their karma, transmigrate and are entrapped. But also introduced in the middle centuries B.C.E. in India and henceforth continuing in all Hindu traditions was the notion that the world of samsara was fundamentally illusory. This doctrine, known as *maya*, "illusion," held that it is because of our own ignorance that we perceive a world of differentiation and change; and it is through our own ignorance that we suffer and produce karma. Samsara is contrasted to an unconditioned, eternal, and transcendent state that is equated with "freedom" or "liberation" from such transience, suffering, and rebirth.

While some version of the doctrine of karma and rebirth has been embraced by some in the modern West as an optimistic alternative to nihilism and the finality of death, in India karma and the transmigration of souls have always been understood as the major religious problem. Karma (in the sense of ritual action) went from being the solution to the problem of evil and suffering in the Vedic period to (in its revised form as action of all sorts) being the principal problem itself in post-Vedic Hinduism. Since the middle of the first millennium B.C.E., Hindu traditions have all faced the same predicament: How can one free oneself from the endless cycle of karma and rebirth? How can one escape the suffering that pervades the world of samsara?

WHY DOES SUFFERING MATTER, AND HOW DO WE DEAL WITH, OR OVERCOME, SUFFERING?

These doctrines were originally put forward by various groups of world-renouncers—some of whom gravitated to heterodox traditions such as Buddhism and Jainism, and some of whom remained in the Hindu fold. In all cases, the pessimism surrounding the value of worldly life that accompanies the doctrines of karma, rebirth, and samsara was counterbalanced by alternatives, methods that were designed to obtain for the practitioner a release from the wheel of phenomenal existence.

In the Upanishads and the later religious and philosophical traditions that center on these texts, suffering is the consequence not only of bad karma but of the ignorance and desire that lead one to produce karma of all sorts. The antidote to evil and suffering is thus wisdom, or jnana.

The path of wisdom requires, first and foremost, that one understand properly the nature of the universe. In the monistic philosophy first encountered in the Upanishads and later forming one of the principal schools of Hindu philosophy, jnana means penetrating the illusory appearance of the world as differentiated and attaining a mystical wisdom of the unitary true nature of the universe and all that is in it. Attaining such wisdom also means a complete transformation of the seeker, itself equated with *moksa*, or "liberation"—liberation from ignorance and also liberation from karma.

True knowledge is the knowledge of the unity and identity of one's true "self" (the *atman*) with the cosmic One, the *brahman*. The "self" and the cosmic One are depicted as unborn, unchanging, and therefore not affected by karma:

Verily, he is the great, unborn Soul, who is this [person] consisting of knowledge among the senses. In the space within the heart lies the ruler of all, the lord of all, the king of all. He does not become greater by good action nor inferior by bad action.

—Brhadaranyaka Upanishad 4.4.22

Wisdom, it is also said, acts as a kind of fire that burns up the accumulated karma of the individual. And, as a radical concomitant of such a doctrine, those who have attained this mystical knowledge and have, in essence, overcome the human condition, are said to be free from the karmic consequences of evil action:

> Its mouth [the "mouth of wisdom"] is fire. Verily, indeed, even if they lay very much on a fire, it burns it all. Even so one who knows this, although he commits very much evil, consumes it all and becomes clean and pure, ageless and immortal. ·
>
> —Brhadaranyaka Upanishad 5.14.8

> So he who understands me—by no deed whatsoever of his is his world injured, not by stealing, not by killing an embryo, not by the murder of his mother, not by the murder of his father.
>
> —Kausitaki Upanishad 3.1

The enlightened individual is one who has, like Nietzsche's superman, gone "beyond good and evil":

> Such a one, verily, the thought does not torment: "Why have I not done the good? Why have I done the evil?" He who knows this delivers himself from these two [thoughts]. For truly, from both of these he delivers himself—he who knows this.
>
> —Taittiriya Upanishad 2.9

The development of wisdom also requires overcoming the very source of karma and the rebirths it provokes: desire. All desires are to be eliminated by the seeker of wisdom, and to this end renunciation of the life of a householder is required:

> On knowing him [the true self], one becomes an ascetic. Desiring him only as their home, mendicants wander forth. Verily, because they know this, the ancients desired not offspring, saying: "What shall we do with offspring, we whose desire is this Soul, this world?" They, verily, rising above the desire for sons and the desire for wealth and the desire for worlds, lived the life of a mendicant. For the desire for sons is the desire for wealth, and the desire for wealth is the desire for worlds; for both these are desires.
>
> —Brhadaranyaka Upanishad 4.4.22

To the end of eliminating desire and mastering the mind and body, a variety of practices involving austerities and self-discipline were developed to reshape human consciousness. Ascetic practices of all sorts were designed to overcome the demands of the body, and meditational techniques were formulated to tame the desires and scattered nature of the mind. In a sense, such traditions embraced such practices as a kind of "good" suffering that helped in the greater enterprise to overcome suffering itself.

For the ascetic, world-renouncing, and yogic traditions of Hinduism, evil and suffering are defined as the human condition. Transcending this condition involves transforming the very nature of the human being—replacing ignorance with true knowledge and eliminating desires of all sorts that create karma and propel one through an endless series of rebirths.

This noble goal was and is, however, outside the capabilities of most humans. In response to the world-renouncing philosophies and traditions that center on jnana, post-Vedic Hinduism also produced teachings that emphasized the importance of life in this world and embraced a new philosophy that valorized action in the world. The centerpiece of the reaction to world-renunciation was the concept of *dharma,* a multivalent term that includes within its semantic range "religion" or "righteousness," but also "duty."

Its opposite, *adharma,* can thus mean both "irreligion" or "evil," and also "doing what is not yours to do." It is in the former sense of adharma, as "irreligious" or "evil," that the following text uses the term in the course of arguing that even if it seems that evildoers are "getting away with it," they will pay for their deeds eventually:

> For an irreligious man, a man whose wealth is dishonestly gained, or a sadist does not achieve happiness here on earth. Even when he is sinking through the practice of religion [dharma], he should not set his mind on irreligion [adharma], seeing how quickly the tables are turned on evil, irreligious men. Irreligious practices do not yield their fruits right away in this world, like a cow, but, turning back on him little by little, they sever the roots of the perpetrator. . . . A man thrives for a while through irreligion; he sees good fortune because of it and he conquers enemies because of it; but finally he and his roots are annihilated.
>
> —Manusmrti 4.170–72, 174

Doing one's dharma meant not only remaining ethical, but also assuming the duties that were proper to one's class or caste and one's stage of life. Performing one's "own duty" (*svadharma*), which was in part defined as that ordained by one's birth into a particular class or caste, was here constituted as "the good." "Your own duty done imperfectly is better than another man's done well. It is better to die in one's own duty; another man's duty is perilous."[4] Thus adharma or "evil" could also refer to doing "another man's duty," or stepping outside the boundaries that were set for you by the class and caste in which you were born. The "confusion of classes, by means of which irreligion, that cuts away the roots, works for the destruction of everything" [Manusmrti 8.353], must be avoided.

Within this ideology centering on caste, "evil" could also mean "pollution" or "impurity." The causes of impurity, which threatened one's caste standing, are many: various bodily functions, contact with death, taking food from a member of a lower caste, or even the mere sight of an "untouchable" could have such a result.

If evil and suffering were caused by ignorance, desire, and karma, all activity—including "good" or religiously ordained activity such as following one's dharma—would seem to ensnare one in the web of karma and rebirth. The texts that extol dharma or dutiful activity in the world deal with this problem by the theory of "stages of life," or *asramas*. Dharma is correlated not only to one's class or caste, but to the period of life one is in. After one undergoes a stage of life as a student, the householder stage begins—and it is here that action in the world, guided by dharma, is indeed mandated. But in one's later life, one is to renounce the world of action and pursue the final goal of liberation from all karma.

This is a somewhat unsatisfactory solution to the problem of karma, holding as it does that one is to spend the bulk of life producing and accumulating karma only to reverse the process in the last stages of one's existence. Furthermore, the mandate to perform one's "own dharma" also entails, for some, that the very performance of one's own duties contradicts a general moral scheme in which some actions are regarded as absolutely wrong. Thus, while generally applicable, dharma requires that, for example, although people of all sorts are to practice nonviolence, the specific duties of one born into the warrior class require violence—which would seemingly necessitate bad karma.

The problem of how to act in such a way that bad karma—or indeed, karma of any sort—is not produced is addressed in one of the classic texts of Hinduism, the *Bhagavad Gita*. While upholding the doctrine of specific duty, or svadharma, it also teaches that such actions should be performed without desire. Since desire is the root cause of karma, desireless action in accordance with one's dharma will have no karmic consequences. Such a person is said to be truly wise, like the world-renouncers, but unlike them does not abandon action but rather performs it in the right way:

> What is action? What is inaction? Even the poets were confused— what I shall teach you of action will free you from misfortune. One should understand action, understand wrong action, and understand inaction too; the way of action is obscure. A man who sees inaction in action and action in inaction has understanding among men, disciplined in all action he performs. The wise say a man is learned when his plans lack constructs of desire, when his actions are burned by the fire of knowledge. Abandoning attachment to fruits of action, always content, independent, he does nothing at all even when he engages in action. . . . Content with whatever comes by chance, beyond dualities, free from envy, impartial to failure and success, he is not bound [by karma] even when he acts.
>
> —*Bhagavad Gita* 4.16–20; 22

The *Bhagavad Gita* is also one of the earliest texts of the Hindu theistic devotionalistic movement known as *bhakti*. For in this text, a personalized and monotheistic deity, Krishna, is presented. The teaching of "desireless action" is in part portrayed as a kind of imitation of God:

> Whatever a leader does, the ordinary people also do. He sets the standard for the world to follow. In the three worlds, there is nothing I must do, nothing unattained to be attained, yet I engage in action. What if I did not engage relentlessly in action?

Men retrace my path at every turn, Arjuna. These worlds would collapse if I did not perform action; I would create disorder in society, living beings would be destroyed. As the ignorant act with attachment to actions, Arjuna, so wise men should act with detachment to preserve the world.

—*Bhagavad Gita* 3.21–25

But, additionally, the *Bhagavad Gita* also represents "desireless action" as sacrificial, with the karmic "fruits" of all acts being given up to God. It is, finally, devotion, or bhakti, to Krishna that the Gita teaches is the way to salvation:

Whatever you do—what you take, what you offer, what you give, what penances you perform—do as an offering to me, Arjuna! You will be freed from the bonds of action, from the fruit of fortune and misfortune; armed with the discipline of renunciation, your self liberated, you will join me.

—*Bhagavad Gita* 9.27–28

The paths of action and wisdom are here included within and superseded by what this text and many subsequent traditions within Hinduism regarded as the supreme path, that of bhakti. The devotionalistic wings of Hinduism, with their array of deities, each one regarded by devotees as supreme, all assume that it is by God's grace that evil and suffering can be overcome and salvation made possible. In some of its forms, the bhakti movement seems to have attracted many low-caste followers and others who had been left out or diminished by caste-oriented Hinduism. The movement's emphasis on simple devotion, humility, and the power of God's grace to redeem even the sinner had obvious appeal: "I am false, my heart is false, my love is false; but I, this sinner, can win Thee if I weep before Thee, O Lord. Thou who art sweet like honey, nectar, and the juice of sugarcane! Please bless me so that I might reach Thee."[5]

The power attributed to bhakti to short-circuit the karmic process is often said to be enormous—and inexplicable. In one myth, a demoness named Putana ("the Stinking One"), who is described as a "devourer of children," takes on a pleasing form and visits the village where the infant god Krishna resided with his mother. Deceived about the demoness's true identity, the mother hands over her child to her:

> Then the horrible one, taking him on her lap, gave the baby her breast, which had been smeared with a virulent poison. But the lord, pressing her breast hard with his hands, angrily drank out her life's breath with the milk.

The demoness dies and resumes her true demonic form. But when her body is put on the funereal pyre, the villagers receive a shock, and the reader learns a lesson about the mysterious ways of God:

> The smoke that arose from Putana's body as it burnt was as sweet-smelling as aloe-wood, for her sins had been destroyed when she fed Krishna. Putana, a slayer of people and infants, a female Raksasa [demon], a drinker of blood, reached the heaven of good people because she had given her breast to Vishnu—even though she did it because she wished to kill him. How much greater, then, is the reward of those who offer what is dearest to the highest Soul, Krishna, with faith and devotion, like his doting mothers? . . . Since they always looked upon Krishna as their son, they will never again be doomed to rebirth that arises from ignorance.[6]

As this myth relates, devotion to God overrides ignorance, karma, and rebirth and delivers the devotee from evil and suffering. The bhakti movement also reinterpreted a long-standing Hindu belief that desire was the product of ignorance and the root of karma, rebirth, and suffering. For in devotionalistic traditions, longing for God—often portrayed in erotic terms—and the pain of separation from the object of desire become the emotional means for ratcheting up one's devotion to fever pitch. At the same time, most devotionalistic cults eschewed the goal of merging with or achieving identity with the object of their devotion, for that would preclude the bliss of remaining distinct while basking in God's love. The poet-saint Mahadevi composed the following, in which her love for the god Shiva is represented in erotic terms, and her ultimate desire is to "have it both ways," to be with him and yet not be with him:

Take these husbands who die,
decay, and feed them
to your kitchen fires!

Better than meeting
and mating all the time
is the pleasure of mating once
after being far apart.

When he's away
I cannot wait
to get a glimpse of him.

Friend, when will I have it
both ways,
be with Him
yet not with Him,
my lord white as jasmine?[7]

Another set of traditions in which desire was reworked from its conceptualization as the ultimate source of human suffering into a religious tool was Tantrism. Esoteric Tantric groups, which came in both Hindu and Buddhist forms, argued that the best way to overcome evil and suffering was to confront them and, under ritual conditions, engage in practices that for the uninitiated would result in the most disastrous karmic ends. Through various meditative and ritual techniques, the Tantric practitioner could "do whatever fools condemn" and rid himself "of passion by yet more passion":

> So, with all one's might, one should do
>   Whatever fools condemn,
> And, since one's mind is pure,
>   Dwell in union with one's divinity.
> The mystics, pure of mind,
>   Dally with lovely girls,
> Infatuated with the poisonous flame of passion
>   That they may be set free from desire.
> By his meditations the sage . . .
>   draws out the venom [of snakebite] and drinks it.
> He makes his deity innocuous,
>   And is not affected by the poison. . . .
> When he has developed a mind of wisdom
>   And has set his heart on enlightenment
> There is nothing he may not do
>   To uproot the world [from his mind]. . . .
> Water in the ear is removed by more water,
>   A thorn [in the skin] by another thorn.
> So wise men rid themselves of passion
>   By yet more passion.[8]

SUFFERING AND EVIL: THE LARGER QUESTION OF ETIOLOGY AND THEODICY

As in all other religions, the various strands that make up Hinduism have had to confront the question of origins: Who or what is responsible for evil and suffering? The candidates in world religions are four: (1) superhuman demonic forces or beings; (2) God; (3) "fate," "time," or some other form of the automatic workings of the universe; or (4) human beings themselves. Hindu traditions have versions of all four of these explanations of the origins of evil and suffering, although some are more common than others.

The explanation Hinduism has least often taken recourse to is to blame demons or the forces of cosmic evil for the faults and sufferings of human beings. In the Vedic period, the "demons" are indeed sometimes targeted as responsible for various aspects of human suffering—illness, premature death, sterility, problems with livestock, etc.—and some sacrifices are designed to propitiate them or combat their influence. More often, however, the demons are portrayed in the Veda not so much as the forces of evil as merely the structural opposites of the gods. "The one invariable characteristic of the gods," writes Wendy O'Flaherty, "is that they are the enemies of the demons, and the one invariable characteristic of the demons is that they are opposed to the gods. . . . The two groups, as groups, are not fundamentally *morally* opposed."[9]

In later Hinduism, this purely structural opposition between gods and demons continues, but one also finds passages in later texts that cast demons in roles that place responsibility for the origin of evil on them. Sometimes one encounters myths that conflate demons and "heretics" (and evil with heresy). Demons are said to have introduced false doctrines such as Buddhism, Jainism, and especially materialism to corrupt the originally pure nature of human beings—with the consequence that heretics and those they converted were led to hell:

> In ancient times, the mortals, being pious through the due performance of their duties, could go to heaven at the mere wish, and

the gods also grew stronger by getting their due share in the sacrifices. Consequently the Daiteyas and Asuras [two classes of demons] could not prevail upon the gods. In course of time two Daiteyas, Sanda and Marka by name, intended to annihilate the gods and performed a dangerous *krtya* [a magic rite or witchcraft meant for destructive purposes], from which came out a dreadful figure called Mahamoha ["Great Delusion"], who had a very dark body resembling a mass of darkness and was extremely fierce, haughty, deceitful and lazy. . . . This Mahamoha, who was *adharma* ["irreligion"] in person and was polluted by pride and other vices, took his position among the people and deluded them in various ways. By his misleading instructions he turned them worthless through infatuation and made them discard their conscience as well as their respective duties enjoined upon them by their castes. . . . Thus they led themselves as well as others to hell.[10]

But it is nevertheless somewhat rare in Hindu mythology to find demons responsible for the corruption and suffering of humankind. This "solution" to the problem of evil—found in its most extreme form in Manichaeanism and other dualistic traditions, and also, to some extent, in the Jewish and Christian notions of Satan—is generally not one favored by Hindu traditions. There is no more or less equally powerful devil to counterbalance a powerful God in any form of Hinduism; demons, while formidable and dangerous, are not usually pinpointed as the ultimate source of evil and suffering among human beings. Rather, as O'Flaherty notes, gods and demons are both simply following their own dharma, their own set of cosmically appointed duties: "Gods and demons are 'separate but equal,' rather like two separate castes; each has his own job to do . . . but there is not immorality in the demons; they are merely doing their job."[11]

The second explanation of the origins of evil and suffering, which places blame on God or the gods, is more common, and can raise some of the problems typical of theodicy in other religions. Why did God (or the gods) make a world in which there is evil and human beings suffer? One Buddhist text raises precisely this question as it satirizes Hindu theism:

> The world is so confused and out of joint, why does Brahma not set it straight? If he is the master of the whole world, Brahma, lord of the many beings born, why in the whole world did he ordain misfortune? Why did he not make the whole world happy? . . . Why did he make the world with illusion, lies, and excess, with injustice? . . . The lord of beings is unjust. There is such a thing as justice, but he ordained injustice.[12]

All strands of the Hindu tradition where the existence of God or gods is posited have had to confront the possibility that it is the divine that is responsible for evil and suffering. As we have seen, in Vedic ritualism the universe as a whole and human beings within it are originally created by a god in a faulty manner, and both the cosmos and humans have a perpetual tendency to return to their defective "natural" state. It is the Vedic sacrifice, ritual acts or karma, that repairs this "evil" and produces the "good." The human condition, given by nature and the god who created it, can be overcome by human ritual activity.

With the rise of world-renouncing and ascetic traditions, which also place a premium on the efforts of human beings to overcome pain and suffering in the world, the phenomenal universe (created by god) is understood as a kind of prison from which one must escape. Human beings—created ignorant of the true nature of reality, deluded by their natural sense and untrained cognitive faculties, and governed by desire that perpetually creates karma and thus casts them time and time again into new births in the world of samsara—are urged to overcome their condition and realize their true nature as identical to the universal One. In the following text, such a self-realized being is portrayed as overcoming not only his own nature but the divine forces that stand in the way, that wish to prevent human beings from becoming identical to the "self" of the gods:

"I am *brahman*"—whoever among gods, sages, or men became enlightened to this, he became it all; even the gods had no power to prevent him becoming thus, for he became their self. But whoever worships another divinity [other than his true self, the *brahman* or cosmic One] is like a sacrificial animal for the gods, and each person is of use to the gods just as many animals would be of use to a man. Therefore it is not pleasing to those [gods] that men should know this.

—Brhadaranyaka Upanishad 1.4.10

The jealousy of the divine ones in the face of human threats to their status is reminiscent of certain myths in Jewish and Christian traditions, although here given a particular Hindu enunciation. Evil—in the text below defined as "sleep, exhaustion, anger, hunger, love of dice, desire for women"—is introduced into human nature to prevent humans from joining the gods in heaven:

The gods and the demons were fighting. The gods created the thunderbolt, which was a man, and they sent it against the demons; it destroyed the demons and came back to the gods. But the gods feared it, and broke it into three pieces, and they saw that the hymns that are divinities were inside this man. They said, "After he has lived virtuously on this earth, he will follow us [into heaven] by means of sacrifice and well-performed asceticism. Therefore, let us act so that he does not follow us; let us put evil in him." They put evil in him—sleep, exhaustion, anger, hunger, love of dice, desire for women.[13]

In other texts, God is also said to be responsible for the creation of the evil and suffering attributed to heresy. In the following myth, the god Vishnu creates "evil" (here equated with death, irreligion, darkness, desire, and passion) out of a part of himself:

That portion of Visnu which is one with death caused created being to fall, creating a small seed of irreligion [*adharma*] from which darkness and desire were born, and passion was brought about. Those in whose minds the seed of evil had been placed in the first creation, and in whom it increased, denied Vedic sacrifices and reviled the gods and the followers of the Vedas. They were of evil souls and evil behavior.[14]

But in many theistic traditions, the creation of heresy and the evils associated with it are the work of a good God who intervenes in the cosmos in order to keep proper distinctions. The following text concerns one of the ten incarnations of the Hindu god Vishnu, the Buddha avatar. Vishnu is here said to take on the form of the Buddha in the Kali Yuga (the "dark age" in which we currently live) and preach a false doctrine (i.e., Buddhism) in order to delude demons, the "enemies of the gods":

When the Kali Age has begun, in order to delude the enemies of the gods, Visnu will be born as the Buddha, son of Ajana. . . . When the enemies of the gods come to know the Vedic rites and begin to oppress people, then he will assume an attractive and deluding form and teach irreligion to the demons in the invisible cities made by Maya ["Illusion"], making them heretics. . . . With words he will delude those who are not deserving of the sacrifice. . . . Homage to Buddha, the pure, the deluder of the demons.[15]

Just as God incarnates on earth when unrighteousness and irreligion become too powerful—the premise of the famous Hindu work the *Bhagavad Gita* (see my contribution to *Sacred Texts and Authority,* an earlier volume in this series)—so too can God intervene when the forces of good are in the wrong hands. In these instances, although God is indeed responsible for the introduction of evil and suffering in the world, God is acting in the best interests of a universe that must be kept in balance.

In certain Hindu traditions, the powers of evil and suffering are embodied in divine figures themselves. Goddesses of disease are figures of devotion; the dreadful goddess Kali, who represents time and death, is worshiped with blood sacrifices. "Evil" here is deified and confronted head-on; worshiping such goddesses gives one the hope that evil and suffering can be pacified by being honored. As David Kinsley writes, Kali's fearsome image "fastens one's attention on those aspects of life that cannot be avoided and must eventually result in pain, sorrow, and lamentation. . . . For man to realize the fullness of his being, for man to exploit his potential as a human being, he must finally accept this dimension of existence."[16] As in Tantric traditions, where one "plucks out a thorn by using another thorn," some Hindu devotionalistic groups have thus chosen to fight fire with fire by centering their devotion on the very forces they fear—and yet must confront.

Some explanations of the origin of evil and suffering posit an alternative to both the creation of them by demons and the attribution of them to God:

When Brahma was thinking about creation, at the beginning of the era, there appeared a creation preceded by ignorance and made of darkness; from it was born fivefold ignorance, consisting of darkness, delusion, great delusion, gloom, and blind-darkness. Seeing that this creation was imperfect, Brahma began to create again. . . . His fourth creation produced creatures in whom darkness and passion predominated, afflicted by misery; these were mankind.[17]

An alternative and prior creation to God's, characterized by ignorance and "made of darkness," limits God's ability to create a world without evil and suffering. No demonic power is responsible for this original creation, but the result is that God is more or less forced to produce human beings who are tainted by it ("in whom darkness and passion predominated, afflicted by misery").

Similarly, other myths of origins portray the introduction of evil and suffering as the natural and inevitable workings of time itself. Stories of the loss of a Golden Age portray human beings as victims of the degenerative nature of cosmic history:

Formally, Prajapati brought forth pure creatures, who were truthful and virtuous. These creatures joined the gods in the sky whenever they wished, and they lived and died by their own wish. In another time, those who dwelt on earth were overcome by desire and anger, and they were abandoned by the gods. Then by their foul deeds these evil ones were trapped in the chain of rebirth, and they became atheists.[18]

Other myths also represent the fall from a primordial time of happiness (and equality) to a time when greed and passions rule without offering any causal explanation save for the passage of time:

In the Golden Age, people were happy and equal. There was no distinction between high and low, no law of separate classes. Then, after some time, people became greedy . . . and passions arose.[19]

In the beginning, people lived in perfect happiness, without class distinctions or property; all their needs were supplied by magic wishing-trees. Then because of the great power of time and the changes it wrought upon them, they were overcome by passion and greed. It was from the influence of time, and no other cause, that their perfection vanished. Because of their greed, the wishing-trees disappeared; the people suffered from heat and cold, built houses and wore clothes.[20]

The cyclical nature of time entails not just an inevitable degeneration of time, with the resulting decrepitude of moral sensibility and the increase in evil and suffering; it also implies an equally inevitable return to the Golden Age as the wheel of time turns once again. The righteous will survive as the seeds for a new and better cosmic era:

In the Kali Age, men will be afflicted by old age, disease, and hunger and from sorrow there will arise depression, indifference, deep thought, enlightenment, and virtuous behavior. Then the Age will change, deluding their minds like a dream, by the force of fate, and when the Golden Age begins, those left over from the Kali Age will be the progenitors of the Golden Age. All four classes will survive as a seed, together with those born in the Golden Age, and the seven sages will teach them all dharma. Thus there is eternal continuity from Age to Age.[21]

It is here the simple "force of fate" that impels the ever-changing world of samsara, characterized by an "eternal continuity" that links the circle of time. Evil and suffering are, from this point of view, the inexorable consequences of the eternal processes that guide the phenomenal universe.

The formulation of a causal and moral "law of karma," at least in its pure form, provides Hinduism with yet another explanation for the origins of evil and suffering. Human beings are responsible for their own destinies, for better or for worse.

Suffering in this life is the direct consequences of evil deeds performed in the past, and suffering in the future will be the direct consequence of evil deeds performed in the present. Some have argued that karma provides Indian traditions (Buddhism and Jainism, as well as Hinduism) with a logical solution to the conundrums of theodicy faced in other religions.

Max Weber, the great sociologist of religion, wrote that "the most complete formal solution of the problem of theodicy [here in the general sense of the existential need to explain suffering and evil] is the special achievement of the Indian doctrine of *karma,* the so-called belief in the transmigration of souls."[22]

But does the law of karma really solve the problem of evil and suffering? Cognitively, it does explain the classical formulation of the problem of justice: Why do good things happen to bad people, and why do good people suffer? But in the absence of memory of past lives, and the deeds done in them that carry good and evil consequences into the present, evil and suffering often seem as random and unprovoked to Hindus as to anyone else. Furthermore, while the law of karma might be, to some degree, a logical intellectual explanation, it is certainly not emotionally satisfying. Few humans, in India or anywhere else, find it palatable to believe that they themselves are responsible for every aspect of their fate.

Hinduism has rarely remained true to the strict workings of the law of karma and the onus it places on human beings for their own suffering and the existence of evil. Outside forces—demons or gods—or the sheer inexorable workings of fate obviate human responsibility; and in theistic traditions an individual's karma can, as we have seen, be overridden by divine grace. Devotional traditions often depend upon such grace to alleviate suffering.

If one can speak of *a* Hindu worldview, it is one that accepts, at least provisionally, the necessity of all opposites—evil as well as good, suffering as well as happiness. All these "pairs of opposites" were created in the beginning and all creatures were "yoked" with them. Every creature, guided by his own "innate activity" or dharma, merely follows his own nature:

> And in order to distinguish innate activities, he [the creator god] distinguished right from wrong, and he yoked these creatures with the pairs, happiness and unhappiness and so forth. For, with the impermanent atomic particles of what are traditionally known as the five [elements], in their order this whole [universe] comes into being. And whatever innate activity the Lord yoked each [creature] to at first, that [creature] by himself engaged in that very activity as he was created again and again. Harmful or harmless, gentle or cruel, right or wrong, truthful or lying—the [activity] he gave to each [creature] in creation kept entering it by itself. Just as the seasons by themselves take on the distinctive signs of the seasons as they change, so embodied beings by themselves take on their innate activities, each his own.
>
> —Manusmrti 1.26–30

While evil and suffering are in Hinduism, as in all other religions, regarded as unfortunate and as problems to be overcome, they are also regarded as necessary to and part of the balance of the cosmos as a whole. But beyond and behind this phenomenal world is true reality, where evil and suffering do not exist. The very existence of the "pairs of opposites" in the world provides the precondition for the struggle to overcome them, whether through ritual or other religious activity, through the cultivation of wisdom and yogic discipline, or through devotion to and faith in a personal god. It is, finally, a state that lies beyond such opposites, beyond good and evil and the karmic mechanism that produces them, that Hinduism posits as the ultimate goal.

CHAPTER 2

Buddhism

WHY ARE EVIL, SUFFERING, AND PAIN
A PROBLEM FOR BUDDHISM?

Over the course of a teaching career that spanned forty-five years, Gautama Buddha (563–483 B.C.E.) taught powerfully and beautifully to many different audiences on a wide variety of topics. But by one account, at least, he refused to acknowledge that there was any significant variety in his message. As he said to one of his students, "Both formerly and now, it is only suffering and the stopping of suffering that I describe" (*Majjhima Nikaya* I.140).

Gautama Buddha's own account of his teaching career also holds good as a description of Buddhism as a global religion. To say this is not to belie the fact that Buddhism, like other religious traditions, is historically complex and internally diverse. For approximately 2,500 years, the Buddha has been the inspiration and focus point for an extraordinarily diverse set of religious aspirations and practices, first in India and gradually across Asia; in the twentieth century, Buddhism has spread around the world, and there are now vibrant Buddhist communities in the Americas, Europe, and Africa, as well as Asia. The complexity and diversity of Buddhist thought and practice, the richness of its character in local settings, are such that when Europeans first encountered Buddhists in their explorations at the beginning of the colonial age, it took them quite a while to re-

alize that the religion they encountered in Sri Lanka was historically related to what they saw in Japan. And yet, amidst all the
diversity and complexity of ideas, practices, experiences, and
values, we can still see that Buddhists share a sustained attentiveness to "suffering and the stopping of suffering."

For Buddhists, suffering is as simple as it is complex. It is
simply "what is hard to bear," but what is hard to bear comes in
an infinite number of guises, from anything that hurts us to
not getting what we want. Suffering includes physical pain, of
course, but also psychological states of distress, such as fear,
worry, and grief; it also includes all forms of social suffering,
such as loneliness and the animosity of others. Existence in
"states of woe," the oppressive and painfully debilitating conditions of certain forms of life, whether they are poverty and prej-
udice among humans, animal life with all its predaciousness, or
birth in the various hells of the Buddhist universe, is also suffering. A learned classification of suffering found in the Theravada
Buddhist canon[1] distinguishes four kinds of suffering in an attempt to encapsulate the complexity of suffering's guises: (1) the
suffering caused by the fact of just being born, and in this category we can see an alertness on the part of Buddhists to suffering among all beings, animal and human, hell-dweller as well as
god; (2) illness and other bodily suffering; (3) physical discomfort that one suffers because of the circumstances that one finds
oneself in, from something as small as a mosquito bite to as
great as a natural disaster like a famine; and (4) the mental and
emotional distresses that occur in and through human relations, from grief after the death of a loved one to worry over
what might happen to a friend. This last category of mental distress also includes the anguish that one may feel over the loss of
property or employment.[2]

Given classifications of this kind, it is not surprising that,
historically, the practice of empirical medicine has been a key
component of the cultural heritage of Buddhism, and medical

skill has consistently been cultivated by Buddhist monks and laypeople. Buddhists also studied and practiced nonempirical forms of healing—what some might want to call magic—with enthusiasm. The following passage from a text from Nepal is about a protective charm, or *dharani,* a way of stopping suffering that appealed to many Buddhists in the past, but the passage also gives us a good idea of the range of suffering that Buddhists thought it necessary to address:

> [The Buddha] turned to those assembled there and said, "Listen, I tell you that the Mahapratisara dharani [the protective charm] is for the welfare and happiness of humanity. Hearing this dharani, one can destroy the cause of whatever distress one is suffering. One who recites this Mahapratisara dharani will be free from harm by demons, monsters, spirits, hungry ghosts, astral divinities, Siva-demons, madness, epilepsy, and dangers from all beings, human and non-human. All one's sworn enemies will be reconciled. One will be immune from the dangers posed by poison, fire, weapons, water, wind, and so on, and will be immune from contagious diseases." [3]

Buddhists have treated mental suffering too with a battery of specific practices, from exorcisms to chanting and meditation, while still other meditative exercises have been deployed against the existential roots of suffering, that is, desire and ignorance. We will postpone considering these existential roots until later in this chapter, when we consider the origin of suffering. It is sufficient to note here that Buddhists have defined the highest goal of their religious lives—to become awakened in the same way as the Buddha did—as the stopping of suffering, and this is done by removing the existential roots of suffering.

Buddhists have been alert not only to their own suffering but to that of others as well, although, sadly, they have done their part to add to the sum of human suffering in history too.

Their efforts at stopping suffering will receive our attention here, although, as we will see below, Buddhist etiologies of suffering allow for no exceptions for evil behavior on the part of Buddhists.

The great Buddhist emperor of ancient India, Ashoka (c. 270–230 B.C.E.), planted trees and dug wells along roadsides to provide shade and refreshment for weary travelers. He also built hospitals for both humans and animals, another instance of Buddhist alertness to suffering being a common denominator among all beings. Ashoka's example has inspired many ordinary men and women to provide rest and comfort for strangers and animals in similar ways, and his efforts at social reform—giving amnesties to those convicted of capital crimes and ending hunting in his kingdom, for example—still inspire contemporary "engaged Buddhists" in their own efforts at peacemaking and social change. Some Buddhists have performed rituals to ease the excruciating pain of hungry ghosts, those unfortunate beings who, because they have exceedingly large stomachs and needle-sized mouths, are constantly in a state of burning hunger, while others, seeking to bring happiness and well-being to others, have chanted the title of the *Lotus Sutra*,[4] one of the most important Buddhist Sutras in East Asia, out of a confidence that "once one chants *nam-myoho-renge-kyo* ['praise to the Lotus Sutra'], that single sound summons forth the Buddha nature inherent in all Buddhas, all laws, all [future Buddhas] . . . and all beings of Hell, Hungry Ghosts, Animality, Angry Titans, Humanity, and Heaven, as well as all living beings. This benefit is incalculable and boundless."[5] A list of the ways that Buddhists have tried to stop suffering would go on and on.

But why is suffering a problem for Buddhists? In some religions—such as the great monotheist religions, Islam, Judaism, and Christianity—suffering (and its conceptual sibling, evil) is a problem because it suggests another problem, one that is theological: If God is good, then where did evil come from? If God is loving, why do we suffer? In these religions, the problem of suffering is a "why" question. What is the meaning of suffering? Why does it exist at all? In Buddhism, however, suffering is a problem in and of itself, and as such, it seems too obvious even to ask why it is a problem. Who would dare ask the person engulfed by the pain of a fatal wound, "What's your problem?" Suffering is something that no one wants and something that no one seeks ordinarily. It is appropriate, however, to ask "how" questions about suffering because they can help us to stop suffering. How do particular instances of suffering come about, so we can avoid them? How can particular instances of suffering be stopped once they have begun? How can suffering itself be stopped?

Suffering is a problem that must be solved, rather than just endured, because suffering produces more suffering. We can see that this occurs in three ways. First, suffering produces more suffering because in this world it is easy to mistake suffering for something else. In Buddhist understandings, suffering is all-encompassing and there is nothing in this world that is not necessarily and adequately described as suffering, even those moments that may feel exquisitely otherwise. Since suffering is intrinsic to every experience in this world, even those that feel pleasant inevitably have their end in pain and distress. This is because the end of a pleasant experience is a source of frustration; there may be more distress if the pleasure cannot be repeated. Suffering's ubiquity is ill-matched to our wishes and fantasies. In fact, we suffer *because* we refuse to recognize the truth about ourselves and the world. Instead, trusting perceptions of ourselves and the world that are tainted by ignorance and desire—especially our wish that suffering not be, and our misplaced confidence that we can somehow skillfully avoid it in this world—we try to live in the world in a manner that is not possible. Of course, we suffer as a result. An illustration of how easy it is for us to misperceive suffering, to avoid acknowledging it as our fate, is found in a parable told by the Buddha in the *Lotus Sutra*. A rich man is said to have a large, beautiful estate with a great mansion. The house is impressive at a distance, but closer inspection reveals its true condition:

> His house is broad and great; it has only one doorway, but great multitudes of human beings, a hundred or two hundred, or even five hundred, are dwelling in it. The halls are rotting, the walls crumbling, the pillars decayed at their base, the beams and ridgepoles precariously tipped. Throughout the house and all at the same time, quite suddenly a fire breaks out, burning down all the apartments. The great man's sons, ten, or twenty, or thirty of them, are still in the house.
>
> The great man, directly he sees this great fire breaking out from four directions, is alarmed and terrified. He then has this thought: "Though I was able to get out safely through this burning doorway, yet my sons within the burning house, attached as they are to their games, are unaware, ignorant, unperturbed, unafraid. The fire is coming to press in upon them, the pain will cut them to the quick. Yet at heart they are not horrified, nor have they any wish to leave."[6]

In this parable, the great mansion is this world, *samsara*, the cycle of death and rebirth; samsara is a conception of the world that Buddhists shared with Hindus. The concerned father who has escaped is the Buddha, and the one doorway out of the house is the path of Buddhist thought and practice, which stops suffering. We are the children in the house, and it is telling that we are portrayed in the parable as children, more full of fun than prudence or awareness. We are so preoccupied with the immediate pleasures of our toys that we do not even see the dangers that are all around us, and thus we do nothing to avoid the pain that will inevitably and quickly be ours. This parable is a vivid illustration of the way in which the momentary pleasures of life distract us from the larger conditions of suffering that characterize the world.

Suffering also produces more suffering because in this world it is easy to deceive ourselves about the nature of our actions, especially when they are causes of suffering. Humans have an incredible capacity to deceive themselves about their suffering —to avoid taking responsibility for their own suffering—and we easily find "good reasons" for the bad actions that we do, but this does not change the suffering that these actions will bring us through the workings of karma, the law of moral cause and effect whereby one gets good by doing good and one receives misfortune by doing evil:

> So-called reasons for making oneself happy are not lacking anywhere at all. Even those people who take pleasure in such evil actions as killing fish and butchering hogs claim that this slaughter of living beings is justified because of their caste. The lord of the people [i.e., the king] imagines that [his executing criminals] is his job and he thinks that there is nothing that is not virtuous about it. In this way, one may create reasons that are satisfying. But the demerit of these actions is not destroyed. It is just the same for the king. Since one observes that mainly he has done evil, he will experience the maturation of that evil in bad rebirths. His heart, overwhelmed by the fire of misery, will break into many hundred of pieces.[7]

A second way that suffering produces more suffering occurs in most of our attempts to avoid pain and distress. Pathetically, we frequently pursue what actually brings pain in our efforts to escape pain. Our efforts to escape pain can cause more pain because we choose courses of action on the basis of wrong notions about ourselves and the nature of the world. One sixth-century Indian Buddhist commentator, Bhavaviveka, put it this way:

[Ordinary people] are like someone who is swept away by a stream and seizes on a river to be saved, only to be swept away more forcefully than before. Ordinary people have sunk in a river of suffering because of previous actions. Trying to extinguish this suffering, they have fallen into a river of suffering: they create even greater hindrances and by these actions seize onto actions that turn into a vast river of samsara. With minds deluded by ignorance they have continued in the stream of samsara to increase the causes of suffering—that is, they hold onto the mental habit of considering this [world] to be real because of passion, rebirth, the false view of the self.[8]

Besides helping us to see that suffering causes more suffering, Bhavaviveka's metaphor helps us to appreciate Buddhist understandings of evil. Suffering, as an experience, is dependent on previous evil, but evil is dependent, as a category, on suffering, and an action is deemed evil because it is the cause of suffering. This means, of course, that judgments about evil are frequently radically situational. What is evil in one situation may not always be in another. This is one way that evil is a problem for human beings—like suffering, it is easy to mistake it for something else.

Bhavaviveka's imagery helps show that we often cause more problems for ourselves and for others in our desperate struggles to escape our problems. The manner in which this occurs is illustrated in a story about one of Gautama Buddha's previous lives, which tells how the future Buddha gave his own body to feed a starving tiger mother; this story is one of the most beloved in the Buddhist world. The tigress is described in the following way in a Sanskrit version of the story from fourth-century India:

There, in a mountain cave, [the future Buddha] noticed a tigress so overcome by the pangs of giving birth that she was too weak to move. Her eyes were hollow with hunger, her belly horribly thin, and she looked upon her whelps, her off-spring, as so much meat, while they, trusting their mother and without a qualm, sidled up to her, thirsty for milk. But she menaced them with ferocious roars, as though they were strangers. The [future Buddha] remained calm at the sight of her, but compassion for another creature in distress made him shake like Himalaya in an earthquake. It is remarkable how the compassionate put a brave face on things when they themselves are in dire trouble—but tremble at others' distress, however slight. Though emotion gave emphasis to his words, the future Buddha spoke to his disciple in tones that by force of pity were subdued but also showed his exceptional character.

My dear boy, look how futile it is, this round of birth and rebirth [samsara]. Starvation forces this beast to break the laws of affection. Here she is, ready to devour her own off-spring. Oh! how fierce is the instinct for self-preservation, such that a mother can be willing to eat her own young. How can one allow this scourge to continue unabated—this self-love which prompts such atrocities? Go quickly and search everywhere to appease her hunger, before she does harm to her young ones or to herself.[9]

The details of this story reveal a lot about Buddhist understandings of suffering. Notice, in contrast to Bhavaviveka, that the story does not explicitly invoke any notion of karma in setting the stage. In this, it is closer to the Theravada classification of four kinds of suffering, which we noted above. The tigress suffers simply because of an extreme condition that began in the natural processes of giving birth. Her suffering is so great, however, that there is a possibility that she will turn to violence and eat her children, overwhelming the restraints of a mother's love, to escape her pain. Suffering begets more suffering: her cubs will suffer immediately, and by the law of karma she will suffer in the future.

Bhavaviveka draws our attention to a third way that suffering produces suffering when he says that beings "increase the causes of suffering [when] they hold onto the mental habit of considering this [world] to be real because of passion, rebirth, the false view of the self."[10] In particular, suffering can reinforce the false view that there is a permanent and essential self, with its attendant notions of "me" and "mine." The idea of a permanent and essential self is both false and pernicious: false because it is wishful thinking that has no supporting evidence and pernicious because it is a source of violence and hatred and thus a cause of suffering. Remember how the future Buddha in the story about the tigress noted that the fierce instinct for *self*-preservation could prompt unusual cruelty. The converse is equally true insofar as seeing that there is truly no self brings an end to suffering:

> When through wisdom one perceives
> "everything is without a self"
> Then one is detached from suffering.[11]

Although being aware that there is no enduring self frees us from suffering, many experiences of suffering make us feel all the stronger that we really do have a self (or a "Self") that defines who we are. It is "I" who feels pain after all, and not neural synapses; it is "I" who asks, in the midst of pain, "why *me*?"; and it is "I" who gives quick assent to the plaint of the African American spiritual, "Nobody knows the troubles *I've* seen." We see an example of Buddhist awareness of the power of suffering to reinforce false ideas about a distinctive self and to encourage us to view the world with our imagined self at its center in the following story of a woman whose only child had died; although the story is found in many parts of the Buddhist world, this version is from fifth-century Sri Lanka and is translated from the Pali language. It is also an illustration of how suffering occurs in and through human relations. This story shows that a mother's love can also cause suffering, in contrast to the story of the tigress, where it could not prevent suffering. Most importantly, however, we see how the Buddha eased this mother's grief by forcing her to discover and to experience for herself that suffering is a common denominator among all people. This experience not only freed her from the sense that she was alone, an individual, in her suffering, it also freed her from her grief itself:

[Kisa Gotami's] child died as soon as he was able to walk. Now Kisa Gotami had never seen death before. Therefore when they came to remove the body for burning, she forbade them to do so. She said to herself, "I will seek medicine for my son." Placing the dead child on her hip, she went from house to house inquiring, "Do you know anything that will cure my son?" Everyone said to her, "Woman, you are stark mad that you go from house to house seeking medicine for your dead child." But she went away thinking, "Surely I shall find someone who will know a medicine for my child. . . ."

[Eventually] she went to the [Buddha] . . . and asked him, "Venerable Sir, is it true, as men say, that you know about a formula for medicine to cure my child." "Yes, I do." "What shall I bring [to make the medicine]?" "A pinch of white mustard seed." "I will, Sir, but from whose house?" "In that house in which neither son nor daughter nor anyone else has yet died. . . ." Then she placed the dead child on her hip, entered the village, stopped at the door of the first house and asked, "Do you have any white mustard seed? They say it will cure my child. . . ." They brought grains of white mustard seed and gave it to her. She asked, "Friends, in your house has a son or daughter died?" "What are you saying, woman? As for the living, they are few; only the dead are many. . . ."

After this manner, she went from house to house. She never

found a house which could provide the mustard seed she sought, and when evening came, she thought: "I thought I alone had lost a child, but in every village the dead outnumber the living." And while she reflected thus, her heart became hard where before it had been soft with a mother's love. She took the child and gave him a funeral in the forest and went back to the Teacher.

[The Buddha] said, "Did you get the single pinch of mustard seed?" "I did not, Venerable Sir." The Teacher said, "You vainly imagined that you alone had lost a child. But all living beings are subject to an unchanging law, and it is this: 'The Prince of Death, like a raging flood, sweeps away all living beings into the sea of ruin; still their longings are unfulfilled.'" [12]

Note the important point that the story makes about how suffering is to be explained: We add to our suffering when we try to live as if we were excepted from "unchanging laws." Like other religious traditions, Buddhism frequently reminds us that the most adequate explanations for suffering are usually not the explanations that we begin with or that we would prefer to hear.

HOW IS SUFFERING REPRESENTED AND PERCEIVED AND EXPERIENCED?

The story of Kisa Gotami illustrates some common ways in which suffering has been represented, perceived, and experienced by men and women in the various Buddhist traditions: as death, as madness, and as aloneness. The last image represents a basic truth, since suffering is always experienced alone and this is why it can reinforce false views of self. The following passage from the Theravada Buddhist canon uses some of this same imagery, even as it reiterates the point in Kisa Gotami's story that otherwise admirable human relations of love and loyalty lead to suffering. This passage also reiterates what we saw in the story of the tigress about how our inept attempts to avoid suffering, motivated by our madness, produce even more suffering:

Once . . . there was a certain man whose wife died. Owing to her death he went mad, out of his mind, and wandering from street to street, crossroads to crossroads, would say, "Have you seen my wife? Have you seen my wife?" From this it may be realized how from a dear one, owing to a dear one, comes sorrow and lamentation, pain, distress, and despair.

Once in this same [city] there was a wife who went to her relatives' home. Her relatives, having separated her from her husband, wanted to give her to another against her will. So she said to her husband, "These relatives of mine, having separated us, want to give me to another against my will," whereupon he cut her in two and slashed himself open, thinking, "Dead we shall be together." And from this it may be realized how from a dear one, owing to a dear one, comes sorrow and lamentation, pain, distress and despair.[13]

The image of suffering as death is a common one among Buddhists, and in fact they trace it back to the life of Gautama Buddha. Gautama's discovery of suffering is symbolized in his biography to his seeing an aged man, a sick man, and a corpse. He also sees an ascetic, and together these four sights prompt Gautama to go in search of "the deathless," a search that culminates in his becoming awakened (i.e., the Buddha) and freed from suffering.

The representation of suffering as death is also found in Gautama Buddha's very first sermon, "The Turning of the Wheel of the Law," where he taught that:

Birth indeed is suffering, old age is suffering, sickness is suffering, death is suffering, being with what is disliked is suffering, not being with what is liked is suffering, not getting what one desires is suffering.[14]

The experience of the sufferings represented in this passage as birth, old age, sickness, and death is elaborately conveyed by Buddhaghosa, a fifth-century commentator and the greatest writer of the Theravada Buddhist tradition, in graphic and concrete terms. A selection from what he has to say about birth as suffering is adequate to give a taste of his style. It is certainly in sharp contrast to a common contemporary American assumption that a child's experience in the womb is far preferable to what is experienced outside it:

> One is not conceived inside a blue or red or white lotus, . . . but on the contrary, like a worm in rotting fish, rotting dough, cesspools, etc., one is conceived in the belly in a position that is below the receptacle for undigested food (i.e., the stomach), above the receptacle for digested food, between the belly-lining and the backbone, which is very cramped, quite dark, pervaded by very fetid draughts redolent of various smells of ordure, and exceptionally loathsome. And on being conceived there, for ten months he undergoes excessive suffering, being cooked like a pudding in a bag by the heat produced in the mother's womb, and steamed like a dumpling of dough, with no bending, stretching, and so on. So this, firstly, is the suffering rooted in the descent into the womb.[15]

This account emphasizes foulness and corruption, images that are key elements in Buddhist representations of suffering. With this account in mind, we can see that death is an evocative image for suffering because of the corruption and foulness that characterize a corpse. A corpse is not something that attracts, nor does suffering. Death is also a powerful symbol for suffering, not only because it involves intrinsic pain and foulness, like birth, but because it shows that all human goods, including life itself, are impermanent. In fact, impermanence, as a basic fact of the world, can be considered as a guise of suffering—what is called "indirect suffering" (*Visuddhimagga* XIV:35)—because it is a basis for suffering. This is why bodily and mental pleasant feelings are characterized as suffering—as a Theravada Buddhist text says, "They are the cause for the arising of suffering when they change" (*Visuddhimagga* XIV:34).

Suffering as impermanence can be represented in many ways. Abstractly, we can speak of the universal laws of change; concretely, we can describe disasters. But however it is portrayed, the universal fact of the impermanence of all things in the world is a source of suffering because it stirs fear and apprehension among people, as we see in the following account from the longer *Description of the Land of Bliss*,[16] one of the canonical texts of the Pure Land Buddhist school in East Asia:

Calamity occurs unexpectedly—floods and fires, robbers, enemies, and creditors. They burn down and wash away, plunder, crush, and destroy everything that human beings have. The poison of apprehension torments them unrelentingly. Anger burns the mind, worry and toil never leave. Feelings become hardened, desires stiffen, but these persons are never able to let go of their apprehension. And it also happens that, because they are broken by such events, their bodies perish, their lives come to an end. Abandoning all that they have, they leave; no one will accompany them.

The noble and the wealthy are also afflicted by these apprehensions, with myriad worries and fears. Their toils and hardships are like those of others. They too suffer from alternating chills and fevers, always gaining only pain.[17]

Note how in the last sentence the imagery of suffering in this passage invokes the concrete example of illness. We have already seen that illness is classified as a distinctive kind of suffering in itself. Illness is a very productive image for suffering, in part because, as we saw in the Kisa Gotami story, our thoughts almost automatically turn to physicians and remedies for illness, something that obviously does not occur when suffering is represented as death. The following verse from a hymn used in Pure Land funerals in East Asia beautifully portrays the Buddha Amitabha as a Great Physician, but it is a hymn that, except for its final words, could be addressed to any Buddha:

> Thou perfect master,
> Who shinest upon all things and all men
> As gleaming moonlight plays upon a thousand waters at the same time!
> Thy great compassion does not pass by a single creature.
> Steadily and quietly sails the great ship of compassion across the sea of sorrow.
> Thou art the Great Physician for a sick and impure world,
> In pity giving the invitation to the Paradise of the West.[18]

Imagery of a remedy for illness is an equally common way of representing the Buddhist life as the way to stop suffering, as can be seen in this comment about Amitabha made by Shinran (1173–1263), one of the greatest Japanese Pure Land teachers:

> The Buddha is filled with pity for [all beings, especially those difficult to save] and heals them, commiserates with and cures them. It is like the wondrous medicine called *manda* curing all illness. Beings of the defiled world—the multitudes possessed of corruption and evil—should seek and think on the diamond-like, indestructible true mind. They should hold fast to the Primal Vow [to save all beings who call on Amitabha], which is the wondrous medicine called *manda*.[19]

Buddhists have been endlessly creative in exploring suffering through metaphors and images in their attempts to understand better their own experiences of suffering. They have also told many stories to each other about examples of suffering, and in profound ways these stories have allowed people to experience their own sufferings with more immediacy and understanding than might otherwise be possible. We can see an example of this in a classic Buddhist story about a woman named Patacara, which was told by many Khmer refugees who arrived in the United States in the 1980s.[20]

Patacara was the daughter of a wealthy man who married her servant against her parents' wishes. She ran away with him and they had two children, each of whom was born in terrible circumstances. Patacara delivered her children on the roadside as she attempted each time to make her way back to her parents' house so that she could give birth under the care of her parents. While she was giving birth to her second son in a rainstorm, her husband was bitten by a snake while he was collecting sticks to built a shelter for her. He quickly died. Patacara tried to continue going to her parents' house alone, to seek their protection, now that she was a widow. She came to a broad river that was deep enough to make it impossible for her to cross carrying both children. Having set the newborn on the riverbank, she crossed the river with her toddler and left him there. When she was in midstream, returning to get the newborn, a hawk swooped down and carried him off, and when she cried out to frighten the bird, the toddler thought she was summoning him and plunged into the river and drowned. Overwhelmed with grief for her husband and children, Patacara continued toward her parents' home, only to learn from a passing traveler that they too had died in an accident. When Patacara heard this news, she lost her mind, discarded her clothes, and wandered naked and crazy. Other people, when they saw her, chased her away, throwing clumps of dirt at her, but eventually she came to Gautama Buddha, who, out of compassion for her, had her brought into the temple and clothed her. He then preached to her about the true nature of the world, whereupon she regained her sanity and achieved insight into the nature of suffering.

Patacara's life, with its dramatic instances of death and grief, madness and homelessness, must have resonated with the experiences of many of the Khmer refugees, after their years of terror and deprivation during the Pol Pot regime in Cambodia. Patacara not only experienced terrible loss, but she is the only survivor among all of her family members—a situation all too familiar to the Khmer refugees. Certain parts of Patacara's story were repeatedly emphasized by refugee storytellers: the loss of her children, her madness, the way people treated her, and particularly her nakedness—events that mark the kind of human vulnerability again too familiar to the refugees. The Buddha's reaction to Patacara, even to her nakedness, is in contrast to that of all others, and it is his compassion that stops her suffering. He stops her suffering in two ways: mundanely and temporarily when he has her clothed, permanently and ultimately when she attains insight because he preaches to her. Patacara's story thus demonstrates that suffering, even of the most tragic kind, is not without relief and in the end suffering *can* be stopped. This must have been part of the appeal of her story for the Cambodian people who told it while they themselves were still in the midst of their own suffering. This story and its appeal to Khmer refugees teaches us a lot about the reciprocal relationship between the representation of suffering and the experience of suffering. When, as was the case with many refugees, reflecting on one's own life proved to be too confusing and too painful, a well-known story about suffering, such as Patacara's, became a crucial means of taking possession of one's own experience.[21]

WHY DOES SUFFERING MATTER, AND HOW DO WE DEAL WITH, OR OVERCOME, SUFFERING?

The story of Patacara reminds us that one is attentive to suffering in order to stop suffering, and we can see the force—indeed the real urgency—of the Buddha's summation of his teaching: "Both formerly and now, it is only suffering and the stopping of suffering that I describe." As we noted at the beginning of this chapter, Buddhists have developed an incredibly wide range of practices to stop suffering. This might lead us to conclude quickly that suffering itself does not matter, that suffering has no value for Buddhists, but such a conclusion is worth pausing over.

It is true to say that for Buddhists suffering as it ordinarily occurs has little value. Suffering in everyday life is not character building, nor is it redemptive, but it does have value when it is part of a spiritual regimen. Shibayama Zenkei, a twentieth-century Zen master, said that he would "never forget the spiritual struggle I had in sheer darkness for three years. I would declare that what is most important and invaluable in Zen training is this experience of dark nights that one goes through with his whole being."[22] This suggests that suffering can be the occasion for experiences and virtues that are highly valued for what they contribute to a human life.

Indeed, a certain amount of suffering is necessary to make us aware that our fantasies are not actually the way we and the world are. In addition, witnessing the suffering of others can help to generate valuable virtues of empathy, pity, and compassion in us. Awareness and compassion are catalysts and pinnacles of the Buddhist religious life.

Let us look first at how suffering can move us to begin the process of developing more-adequate perceptions of ourselves and the world. Remember, as we saw above, that suffering can actually reinforce false views about the self, but, in a paradoxical way, the awareness that there is actually an alternative to suffering also emerges in the experience of suffering itself:

> At the moment when suffering is known, [the existence of]
>   happiness is known too,
> when existence is known, non-existence is also known.
> When hot is known, so is cold,

When the threefold fire of defilements is known, so their
　　elimination is immediately desired (*Buddhavamsa* IIA.11).
Just as a man scorched by the sun is attracted to the shade . . . , the
sufferer in samsara seeks *nirvana* (liberation).[23]

It is not the case, however, that the converse is true, and
suffering is usually not acknowledged immediately in momentary experiences of pleasure. This is largely common sense: in
the middle of pain, we cling to the possibility of its ending, but
in the middle of pleasure, we rarely attend to the suffering that
will occur when our pleasure ends. Suffering thus is a cause for
a good, something valuable, insofar as it motivates us to seek its
end, to find a way to stop it.

For those beings in the traditional Buddhist cosmos who experience far more pleasure than suffering, such as gods in various heavens, their great pleasure is an obstacle to the stopping
of suffering. The lives of Buddhist gods lack most of the defin-
ing elements of suffering—aging, illness, being with what is
disliked, not being with what is liked, not getting what one
wants. In fact, they only experience birth and, most significantly, death. Like the children in the *Lotus Sutra*'s parable of
the burning house, the gods of the Buddhist heavens amuse
themselves with the various delights and pleasures surrounding
them, but they do nothing to stop or to avoid the suffering that
awaits them, whether by doing good actions that will give them
more pleasure in the future by the workings of karma—this is
the way they were reborn in heaven in the first place—or by
eliminating desire and ignorance, the only way to stop suffering
permanently. When gods are close to death, signs appear on
their bodies that warn them of what is about to come. These
signs all reveal impermanence and corruption, natural facts of
existence in samsara from which life in heaven protected
them—the flowers around them lose their fragrance, their
clothes become drab, sweat appears on their bodies, and their

seats become uncomfortable. And then, "whereas they had been happy, they are no longer happy . . . and they become tired, suffer discomfort in their hands and feet, and become restive."[24]

In this respect, we can see that suffering contributes to human flourishing because its moderate presence—in mild illness, in the gradual signs of aging, in all-too-common daily frustrations, such as is found in human life—gives us constant reminders that we should do something to stop suffering in our own lives, especially before death befalls us. And thus it is that in the traditional Buddhist universe, only humans can become awakened.

Suffering is also a catalyst for the generation of compassion, a crucial element in overcoming both one's own pain and distress and that of others. We saw this acknowledged in the story of the starving tigress when the future Buddha shook like a mountain in an earthquake at the sight of her torment and in Shinran's comment that Amitabha Buddha "is filled with pity for [all beings, especially those difficult to save] and heals them, commiserates with and cures them." Compassion is a key Buddhist virtue, and as the eighth-century Indian Buddhist Kamalashila said, "one should practice compassion from the very outset, for we know that compassion alone is the first cause of all the qualities of Buddhahood":

> Now this compassion grows through an increasing concern for beings who suffer; and thus [one] should meditate upon these beings that throughout the Triple World they are ever tormented with the three-fold suffering of their condition.[25]

Buddhaghosa, the fifth-century Theravadin scholastic, gives some instructions on how one should cultivate compassion in meditation in the graphic style we saw above:

One who wants to develop compassion should begin his task by reviewing the danger in lack of compassion and the advantage in compassion. . . .

In the *Vibhanga* [a Theravada canonical text] it is said, "And how does a monk dwell pervading one direction with his heart endued with compassion? Just as he would feel compassion on seeing an unlucky, unfortunate person, so he pervades all beings with compassion." Therefore, first of all, on seeing a wretched man, unlucky, unfortunate, in every way a fit object for compassion, unsightly, reduced to utter misery, with hands and feet cut off, sitting in the shelter for the helpless with a pot placed before him, with a mass of maggots oozing from his arms and legs, and moaning, compassion should be felt for him in this way: This being has indeed been reduced to misery; if only he could be freed from this suffering![26]

SUFFERING AND EVIL: THE LARGER QUESTION OF ETIOLOGY AND THEODICY

Note that both Kamalashila and Buddhaghosa encourage meditation on imagined suffering. There is an important lesson here. Witnessing real suffering is not an appropriate occasion to generate experiences and cultivate virtues, no matter how valued these might be. Real suffering demands a quick and pragmatic response, like the Buddha's when he had Patacara clothed. Real suffering demands action; meditation on imagined suffering is one way that we prepare ourselves to respond appropriately and empathetically to real suffering.

The demands that real suffering makes on us for quick and effective responses shape Buddhist attitudes toward theoretical explanations of why suffering occurs. There is a category of questions in the Buddhist tradition that are considered useless to ask. Gautama Buddha refused to answer the questions of a monk about, among other things, whether the world is eternal, whether it was finite, whether an awakened person existed after death. Gautama Buddha said that he saw no need to answer such questions, and all he thought necessary to teach was the way to stop suffering. To refuse to accept what the Buddha offered until such questions were answered would, he said, be like a man mortally wounded by an arrow who refused to have it removed until he knew the name and other personal particulars of the man who shot him. To insist on having an origin of suffering in general would be to make a similar mistake. We can grasp the point here with the familiar image of illness. Searching for a global cause of suffering would be like expecting a global etiology for illness, one that would explain *why* we get sick in the first place. Such an explanation would be of some theoretical interest, but it would be of little help in curing a particular illness. A more modest etiology of a particular illness, one that identified and named its specific causes, would have far greater value for that purpose.

Even though Buddhists have not been much concerned with global theories that give some significance to the existence of suffering, they have taken considerable interest in pragmatic and particular etiologies of suffering. One of these is karma, which we have already mentioned a few times in this chapter. For Buddhists, even though the world, as the cycle of death and rebirth, is defined by suffering and impermanence, it is also fundamentally orderly in its processes. Just as there are orderly natural processes, so there is an orderly moral process, and the latter gives this world of suffering a just character. *Karma* is the name given to the order by which justice is administered in the world. Through an impersonal law of moral cause and effect, good actions result in good results, bad actions in bad results. No suffering occurs that is not deserved, although the world is sufficiently opaque and our ignorance is sufficiently deep that we usually feel otherwise, and we feel justified, albeit wrongly, in protesting the suffering that happens to us on the grounds of our innocence. The law of karma, like the processes of digestion in our bodies, does not require a god or any other agent to administer it. It is a causal process that is conceptualized on the analogy of other natural processes, and just as we become sick when we eat tainted food, so when we do an evil action we and we alone must suffer the results:

> That spot in the world is not found,
> Neither in the sky nor in the ocean's depths,
> Nor having entered into a cleft in mountains,
>> Where abiding, one would be released from the bad deed.[27]

The complicated workings of karma presuppose that humans and all other beings have multiple lives, and that we can be born in a variety of conditions according to the amount of suffering that we deserve because of our previous actions. In the past, most Buddhists would have accepted that these conditions included heavens and hells, references to which we have already seen, yet there are many contemporary Buddhists who would implicitly restrict the effects of karma only to human life. But there are ample opportunities to see the workings of karma in the many inequities of human life. Some of these inequities and their causes are specified by Nichiren (1222–1282), an influential Japanese Buddhist leader, in one of his letters:

> The *Hatsunaion* Sutra reads, "Men of devout faith, because you committed countless sins and accumulated much evil karma in the past, you must expect to suffer retribution for everything you have done. You may be reviled, cursed, with an ugly appearance, be poorly clad and poorly fed, seek wealth in vain, be born to an impoverished or heretical family, or be persecuted by your sovereign. . . ." One who climbs a high mountain must eventually descend. One who slights another will in turn be despised. One who deprecates those of handsome appearance will be born ugly. One

who robs another of food and clothing is sure to fall into the realm of hungry ghosts. One who mocks noble men or anyone who observes the [Buddhist moral] precepts will be born to a poor family. One who slanders a family that embraces the True Law [of Buddhism] will be born to a heretical family. One who laughs at those who cherish the [Buddhist moral] precepts will be born a commoner and meet with persecution from his sovereign. This is the general law of cause and effect.[28]

There is a relatively basic etiology here—like produces like—but it is sufficient to enable us to choose actions that will produce desired conditions and avoid actions that will produce conditions of suffering in the future. Unfortunately for us, bad action is weightier in its results than good and it is far easier to produce suffering than to produce pleasure. This is so for a number of reasons. First, in the workings of karma, evil action has exponentially large bad results, while good actions do not; that is, we gain more suffering from one bad action than we gain pleasure from one good action. Among the results of karma are some of our most basic psychological dispositions—karmic constituents—such as a propensity to be impulsive, angry, pessimistic, etc., and these dispositions shape the choices of our actions; some karmic constituents obviously can predispose us to do bad actions, which will produce even more suffering in the future. Moreover, as was indicated in the story of the starving tigress, suffering produces suffering because when we find ourselves in conditions of suffering, we are more apt to engage in actions that will generate even more suffering. Finally, suffering seems inevitable in samsara because, as Nichiren suggested when he said that "one who climbs a high mountain must eventually descend," it is impossible to live in samsara and experience only pleasure as the result of our karma. As we have seen, the conditions for creating future suffering are always at hand.

In the end, the only way to stop suffering, rather than just temporarily avoid or assuage it, is to eradicate its most fundamental causes. This brings us to the most important etiologies of suffering in the Buddhist traditions. They are connected to ideas of karma because in Buddhism it is the thought that counts most when it comes to karma, and the most fundamental causes of suffering are to be found in human psychology:

If, with perception polluted, one speaks or acts,
Thence suffering follows
    As a wheel the draught ox's foot.[29]

Gautama Buddha identified one of the fundamental causes of suffering in his first sermon when he taught the Four Noble Truths:

This, monks, is the Noble Truth of Suffering: birth is suffering; decay is suffering; illness is suffering; death is suffering; presence of objects we hate is suffering; separation from objects we love is suffering; not to obtain what we desire is suffering. . . .

This, monks, is the Noble Truth concerning the Origin of Suffering: verily, it originates in the craving which causes the renewal of becomings, is accompanied by sensual delight, and seeks satisfaction now here, now there; that is to say, craving for pleasures, craving for becoming, craving for not becoming.

This, monks, is the Noble Truth concerning the Cessation of Suffering: verily, it is passionlessness, cessation without remainder of this very craving; the laying aside of, the giving up, the being free from, the harboring no longer of, this craving.

This, monks, is the Noble Truth concerning the Path which leads to the Cessation of Suffering: verily, it is this Noble Eightfold Path, that is to say, right views, right intent, right speech, right conduct, right means of livelihood, right endeavor, right mindfulness, and right meditation.[30]

We learn from the Four Noble Truths not only that suffering exists and that it can be stopped, but that it has a cause that, once known, allows us to take steps to stop suffering. Suffering is caused by desire, and we will be able to stop suffering in a permanent way only when we are able to stop desire. Those happy people who cease to desire life itself will not be reborn and they will experience no more suffering in future births.

Ignorance as a fundamental cause of suffering is implicit in the formulation of the Four Noble Truths. Desire is a cause of suffering because our desires are shaped by our misperceptions of the world. Ignorance as a fundamental cause of suffering is explicitly acknowledged in one of the other great etiologies of suffering found in the Buddhist world: the doctrine of interdependent origination. In the following passage from the Theravada canon, a member of another religious movement questions Gautama Buddha about the origin of suffering. Note how intimately the discussion is connected to karma:

> "Good Gautama," Kassapa began, "is the suffering that one suffers caused by oneself?"
>
> "No, it is not, Kassapa," replied the Blessed One.
>
> "Then is the suffering that one suffers caused by someone else?"
>
> "No, it is not, Kassapa."
>
> "Well, then, is it caused both by oneself and by someone else?"
>
> "No, it is not, Kassapa."
>
> "Well, then, . . . does it arise spontaneously?"
>
> "No, it does not."
>
> "Then suffering is nonexistent, good Gautama."
>
> "No, Kassapa, it is not nonexistent; there *is* suffering."
>
> "But you do not know it, nor do you see it?"
>
> "Not so, Kassapa, I both know it and see it."
>
> "Good Gautama, to all these questions that I have asked you . . . you have answered no. So please tell me, please teach me about suffering."

"Kassapa, if you say, 'The same individual who does a deed experiences its results'—what you called 'suffering caused by oneself'—then you fall into the view of eternalism [i.e., the individual self is eternal]. But if you say, 'One individual does a deed and another experiences its results'—what a sufferer would call 'suffering caused by another'—then you fall into the view of annihilationism. Kassapa, avoiding these two extremes, the [Buddha] teaches the [Truth] in the manner of a Middle Way:

"Conditioned by ignorance are karmic constituents; conditioned by karmic constituents is consciousness; conditioned by consciousness is individuality; conditioned by individuality are the six senses;[31] conditioned by the six senses is [sensory] contact; conditioned by contact is feeling; conditioned by feeling is desire; conditioned by desire is clinging; conditioned by clinging is becoming; conditioned by becoming is rebirth; conditioned by rebirth are old age, death, sorrow, lamentation, suffering, depression, and dismay. In this way, this whole great heap of suffering originates.

"But from the complete cessation and dissipation of ignorance comes the cessation of karmic constituents; and from the complete cessation of karmic constituents comes the cessation of consciousness [and so forth until] from the complete cessation and dissipation of rebirth comes the cessation of old age, death, sorrow, lamentation, suffering, depression, and dismay. In this way, this whole great heap of suffering ceases."[32]

Key for us in this passage are the last two paragraphs. The first provides an etiology of suffering that explains how desires themselves arise in our bodies, sense perceptions, feelings, and consciousness: desires are dependent on the presence of ignorance. Ignorance, then, is the second fundamental cause of suffering. Ignorance, however, is not a "first cause," but is itself dependent on the fruits of actions in the past that were done out of misbegotten desires.

The second paragraph indicates that this etiology is thoroughly pragmatic. When we eradicate desire or ignorance, we bring to an end "this whole great heap of suffering." The history of Buddhist thought and practice is the complicated record of the various concrete ways that Buddhists have interpreted the fundamental causes of suffering—desire and ignorance—and how they thought these causes could be eradicated. Buddhists have disagreed about the nature of ignorance especially, and they have debated which methods best stop suffering, but they have been consistent in affirming both that suffering can be stopped and that it is worthwhile stopping suffering because to do so brings happiness.

The sheer joy of how it feels to stop suffering can be heard in the autobiographical comments of Nakayama Momoyo, a quite ordinary twentieth-century Japanese woman who began to practice Zen meditation after the death of her son in the Second World War. We begin at a point where she describes her desperate condition, and her story echoes what we have already seen in the story of Kisa Gotami:

> The day I can never forget arrived! May 7, 1945: while I still held in my hands the news of my son's death in battle, his remains were ceremoniously delivered. The agony and grief I felt as I held in my arms the small box of plain wood cannot be expressed with such phrases as "I felt like vomiting blood," or "my heart was broken." Only another mother who has experienced it can know.
>
> I was pushed from a world of light into a world of gloom. I lost all desire to live; every bit of happiness was taken away in grief and hopelessness. A soulless puppet, I mourned day in and day out, wretched with the loss of my son. How many times did I decide to follow my beloved son in death? In my need, I could clearly hear the longed-for voice of my son come back to me: "Mother, you must not die! Please, be happy! Please, live in happiness!"
>
> So my son would not permit me to die, suffer, or sorrow. But I . . . would cry until I was emptied. People criticized me as a fool-

ish mother, a prisoner of my emotions. I fell to a very low place. I felt it would be best if my life would end. I cried on and on for over three years. . . .

On June 3, 1949, I met the nun-teacher Nagasawa Sozen . . . and listened to her give a talk. At first I thought, "How could she understand this pain, this suffering? She's never given birth to a child or raised a child, much less had a child be killed." My hard heart was shut tight, leaving me without a soul in the world to turn to. However, as I listened to the talk and was touched by her character, I felt somehow that there was dragged out from me some kind of innocence free of poison which was just on the other side of my deep and relentless bitterness.

Nakayama Momoyo began to study and practice under the Zen nun-teacher she had met, but her efforts to stop her suffering were themselves painful, much in the spirit of the comments by Shibayama Zenkei quoted above: "During the retreats, my pain and sorrow, my melancholy and wretchedness were beyond words; those who haven't had this experience cannot know what I suffered." But eventually, although with many setbacks too, she made progress in her meditations until:

This greatest of treasures, which I hold, is without a shred of false-hood . . . ; no one could ever harm it. This treasure which I hold, transcends death; even the teacher herself could never damage or destroy it. . . .

Words cannot express what it is like to live and work together with my dead son. . . . My life is full in this vast, delightful and pure world. In one of the teacher's lectures she spoke the lines,

My clear dew mind

Is a ruby

When amongst the autumn leaves.

It's because my mind is clear or colorless that it can adapt to any and all circumstances.[33]

It seems reasonable that we can end by letting Nakayama Momoyo stand for all of Buddhism, even with all the historical complexity of its traditions. Buddhists have been so consistent in their attentiveness to suffering in all its varieties and in all its victims that we can responsibly speak of their religion as simply *shantikarma,* action that brings about peace, and we can see that in the lives of some men and women, like Nakayama Momoyo, it does.

CHAPTER 3

Christianity

WHY ARE EVIL, SUFFERING, AND PAIN A PROBLEM FOR CHRISTIANITY?

A single, determinative choice, made during the second century c.e. and confirmed in countless ways ever since, has made evil a pivotal concern within Christianity. The Apostles' Creed, which emerged during the second century to articulate the rule of faith (as we saw in *Sacred Texts and Authority,* an earlier volume in the Pilgrim Library of World Religions), began "with an embrace of the God of Israel as creator and with an equally emphatic (if indirect) rejection of any dualism which would remove God from the realities of our world."[1] Expressed in that way, the emphasis falls on the reality of Christ's appearance in human flesh, and on Christ's capacity to transform human life in the flesh into the image of God. And that is indeed the incarnational emphasis which governs the Creed, as we also discussed in the earlier volume. But that statement of belief in "God the Father Almighty, maker of heaven and earth" obviously also involves a commitment to the experience of this world as actually attesting the presence of God.

No one needs someone else's list to think of many different ways in which our experience of the world does just the opposite of attesting the presence of God. What are we to make of the suffering of the innocent? Or of the prosperity of the wicked? Of disease and disaster, famine and war, crime and accident? All those and more are part of the experience we hear of every day, and which we all come to know directly, at least in part. The fact of our human mortality carries innumerable forms of suffering and pain with it, and that would seem to make it extremely difficult to understand how God, as a loving and merciful father, can have created a world so riven with evil. The problem is not just the imperfection of what we see around us, but the seemingly unanswerable claim that this world attests evil at least as much as it witnesses to good as its source.

But there were many different options during the second century for viewing the world and the evil within it. What brought the church to the Creed, and then what made for the appeal of the Creed within the church, was not any naive embrace of this world as being inherently good or pleasant through and through. The second century, in fact, brought with it powerful incentives, both intellectual and practical, to deny that God was directly responsible for this world.

The broad appeal of Gnosticism during the second century shows how appealing it could be to abstract God from the world around us. Instead, it could be argued, some other force was in command of the events we all confront, and most fear to confront. The physical circumstances of existence were portrayed by Gnostics as a sham, a fake creation developed by a false god, far removed from the actual Father who provides us with our spiritual being. Although Gnosticism was a remarkably diverse phenomenon, this belief in a fake creation was an underlying feature that united the various factions. This feature is worth emphasizing, because it is frequently not accounted for, and is even ignored, in modern accounts of Gnosticism. There is a tendency to treat Gnostics as if they were simply some sort of liberal thinkers in antiquity, when in fact they insisted that only they had the knowledge (the *gnosis*) to discover and maintain spiritual existence in the face of the claims of a false world.

A good example of a Gnostic text from the second century is
The Gospel of Truth, which begins:

> The gospel of truth is a joy for those who have received from the
> Father of truth the gift of knowing him, through the power of
> the Word that came forth from the fullness—the one who is in the
> thought and the mind of the Father, that is, the one who is ad-
> dressed as the Savior, that being the name of the work he is to per-
> form for the redemption of those who were ignorant of the Father,
> while the name of the gospel is the proclamation of hope, being
> discovery for those who search for him.

What is useful about this initial introduction is that it is a very
simplified summary of the major precepts and assumptions of
Gnosticism.

"Knowledge" here comes only as a gift of the Father, and is
mediated by the "Word," a designation for Jesus taken from the
first chapter of John's Gospel. But that Word comes forth not
directly from God, but from "the fullness," emanations outward from the Father. The complexity of the divine world
around the Father is often elaborated in Gnostic texts, and developed to a bewildering degree of detail. The fascination with
schemes representing the generation of the world is probably an
inheritance from Greek and Roman mythology. The mastery of
that detail is held to mean that one has successfully become one
who knows, a Gnostic.

A firm distinction is made in *The Gospel of Truth* between
those who are spiritual—capable of receiving illumination—
and those who are material—ignorant of what is being offered
(see *Gospel of Truth* 28–31). Failure to attain *gnosis*, then, is a
mark of one's incapacity to be rescued from the conditions of
this world. The assumption throughout is that the material
world is a pit of ignorance and decay, from which the Gnostic
must be extricated. That explains what is otherwise a puzzling

feature of Gnosticism: the wide variance between ascetical self-denial and the encouragement of libertine behavior. In both cases, freedom from what is material was being claimed and put into practice.

Why should such a pessimistic teaching have been popular? First, it is to be stressed that the actual experience of pain, endemic to the human condition (especially before the development of modern medicine), acutely raises the issue of whether we should attribute what we experience directly to the same, good God who endows us with spiritual consciousness. But that is only the general background against which a world-negating attitude might emerge. What made Gnosticism so appealing just when it succeeded, during the second century C.E.? It can be no coincidence that, in the Greco-Roman world of letters, Stoic philosophy was making great headway at the same time. Marcus Aurelius, the Roman emperor, produced his *Meditations*, in which he sets out a practical scheme for disciplining a rational soul within a changing social and natural world.[2] That fundamental division between the logic of reason and the chaos of experience was characteristic of Stoicism. In the case of the emperor Marcus Aurelius, that led to his dispensing various sorts of advice, such as that one should commit suicide only after a reasoned consideration of the circumstances of one's life, not—as in the case of the Christians—out of simple obstinacy (*Meditations* 11.3).[3] The growing conviction that the rational and the experiential were the opposite ends of a dichotomy was typical of this period, and this accounts for the appeal of Gnosticism, and for the pressure on Christianity to conceive of the world as under the sway of evil.

The other source of pressure to the same effect was much more practical. Although the persecution and torture of Christians for their faith was not routine, it was frequent. Writing around 116 C.E., the Roman historian Tacitus reports how the emperor Nero blamed the Christians for a great fire in Rome (in the year 64), and then saw to their torture and execution with the utmost cruelty. Tacitus held no sympathy for Christianity, which he regarded as an irrational superstition, but he was disgusted by Nero's policy.[4] One reason for his disgust was pragmatic: cruelty arouses pity for the victim, and so is counterproductive. Nonetheless, until the acceptance of Christianity as a legitimate religion under Constantine, the confession of the faith could and often did involve grotesque forms of persecution, torture, and death.[5]

Yet the same Paul who would die in Rome during Nero's pogrom against Christians could insist as late as 57 C.E. in his letter to the Romans (13:1–2):

> Let every person be subject to the governing authorities. For there is no authority except from God, and those that exist have been ordered by God. Therefore one who resists the authorities resists what God has appointed, and those who resist will incur judgment.

Peter is said to have died in the same pogrom (crucified, rather than beheaded, as it is said Paul was),[6] and yet the letter called First Peter (composed around 90 C.E., during another period of persecution) attributes the following advice to him (4:19):

> Therefore let those who suffer according to God's will do right and entrust their souls to a faithful Creator.

There was every intellectual and practical reason to deny that current experience comes from God. Gnosticism (including Gnostic Christianity) offered the possibility of denying the theological legitimacy of the ruling powers, and therefore of accommodating to practically any form of words they might demand. Yet that is exactly what the early Christians did *not* do.

There is a particularly poignant passage from what is called

"The Acts of the Scillitan Martyrs," in which a Roman judge attempts to reason with some people who have been denounced for their Christianity, but are not guilty of any other crime. He explains to them, very patiently, that they can easily walk away from the court, simply by burning some incense before an image of the emperor and swearing an oath of allegiance to him as God's son. His patience extends to a conscientious recognition that the act does not actually require belief: only conformity to the due form is required. Many Gnostic Christians would have had no difficulty complying with the judge's request, and no doubt there were other early Christians who were loyal to the Creed but who nonetheless went along with such friendly advice. But, to the judge's exasperation, the Scillitan martyrs force the judge to condemn them to death, which he eventually does. To his mind (as to that of Marcus Aurelius), they were obstinate. Christians were proud of such behavior in their ranks, and produced an entire literature of martyrdom.

The insistence in 1 Peter 4:19 provides the key to this Christian persistence (or obstinacy, depending upon one's point of view). The fact of God's creation of this world seals it as ultimately good, no matter what our immediate experience of it might make it seem. The beginning of the passage makes its perspective clear (1 Peter 4:12–13):

> Beloved, do not be surprised at the fiery ordeal that is taking place among you to test you, as though something strange were happening to you. But rejoice insofar as you are sharing Christ's sufferings, so that you may also be glad and shout for joy when his glory is revealed.

God's creation of this world in First Peter, in the New Testament as a whole, and in the rule of faith as articulated in the Creed is not to be understood simply as a theoretical expression of where things originally came from. Of course, Christians understand and have always understood that God is good and that what God made (and makes) is very good, in the unmistakable assertion of Genesis 1:31. But they do not say on that basis that what seems bad is really good, or that evil is merely illusory or the work of some other power. Instead, they see present experience as in the process of a transformation, sometimes a painful transformation, in which all goodness (including God's) will be vindicated. Christian faith in creation is more eschatological than anything else: it is concerned with what will happen at the end (the *eskhaton* in Greek) of all things.

Because Christianity is committed to eschatology as the single perspective that makes sense of human experience, it has been obliged to spell out for itself what its eschatology means and how the anticipated transformation of the world is to be worked out. Three types of eschatology have characterized Christianity over time, and they are closely related to one another. All three of them have been represented at any one time, although during a given period there is usually a commitment to one of the types more than the others. Which of the three types is emphasized has a profound impact on how a person and a community deal with suffering, and on how they actually perceive pain. For that reason, the distinctions among the three—and their relationship to one another—are quite important to understand.

Temporal Eschatology

By its very nature, eschatology must involve the end of time as we know and conceive of time. But there is no actual necessity that eschatological expectation should develop into what is defined as an apocalyptic expectation. After all, Jesus instructed his disciples to pray, "Your kingdom will come,"[7] without giving a precise indication of when that moment was to come. Apocalyptic thought involves the claim to understand the sequence and timing of the ultimate events in human affairs, up until and including the end.

Jesus does not appear to have taught any single apocalyptic scheme, and it is even said that, after his resurrection, he explicitly told his followers that "it is not for you to know the times and periods which the Father has set by his own authority" (Acts 1:7). But the fact is that, even without Jesus' encouragement, apocalyptic calendars thrived in primitive Christianity, as evidenced in New Testament books such as the Revelation of John, Second Thessalonians, Second Peter, and Jude, all of which were produced near the end of the first century. There is no single such calendar, so it seems obvious that Jesus did not endorse any one apocalyptic scheme. But then, the variety of the calendars shows how vibrant and diverse apocalyptic expectation was.

Although other forms of eschatology have tended to overshadow temporal eschatology in the subsequent history of the church, there have been notable examples of renewed apocalyptic fervor, especially during times of extreme social change. Examples include the Anabaptists during the Reformation in Europe, and groups such as the Shakers in the United States during the nineteenth century. Today, denominations such as the Jehovah's Witnesses represent the tradition of apocalyptic eschatology.

Transcendent Eschatology

Because thought in the modern (and the so-called postmodern) world is, on the whole, not eschatological, it is easy to dismiss eschatology as a primitive and outdated view of the world. The scientific thought of ancient Greece, which has deeply influenced our own view of science, often conceived of physical reality as static and unchanging, and that has inclined us to prefer views of the world that are also static. Now, however, science itself shows us just how conditional human existence is. Physically, not even the universe appears permanent; solid matter seems to be a myth; the very survival of human beings is called into question by the rapid extinction of many other animal and plant species.

Just as our own world has started to seem less stable and unchanging to us, the world of ancient eschatology has proven to be much less simplistic and "primitive" than was once thought to be the case. It was fashionable a century ago to depict eschatology as a strictly temporal teaching, as if time were its only concern. We have just seen that some eschatology is indeed temporal in its emphasis. But to see God as final in human affairs also involves seeing God's kingdom as working now, transforming the very environment in which we live. As Jesus put it, the kingdom of God "is like yeast, which a woman takes, hides in three measures of dough, until the whole is yeasted" (Luke 13:21; Matthew 13:33). Because space, as well as time, is a dimension of God's activity, eschatology also involves seeing God at work now in God's final revelation, and it involves the possibility of joining God in his kingdom.

The point of the revelation of the kingdom within our world is that it points beyond our world. The kingdom is transcendent: it comes from outside us, transforms us, and directs us outside ourselves. No theologian emphasized this aspect of eschatology more forcefully or influentially than Origen, who taught and wrote (first in Egypt, then in Palestine) during the third century. He died as a consequence of wounds he received during torture under the emperor Decius (who authorized persecution in 249–250 C.E.). In order to explain the value of the promises that are ours in Christ, Origen cites John 17:14, when Jesus asserts that neither he nor his disciples are of the world, and Origen then goes on to explain (*On First Principles* 2.3.6):

> But there is no doubt that the Savior refers to something more glorious and splendid than this present world, and invites and

incites all who believe in him to direct their course towards it. But whether that world, which he wishes us to know of, is one that stands apart and separate from this world in space and quality and glory, or whether, as seems more likely to me, it excels in quality and glory but is nevertheless contained within the limits of this world, is uncertain, and in my opinion an unsuitable subject for the mind and thoughts of human beings.

Origin here expresses a characteristic feature of Christian teaching concerning transcendence. The point is not to speak of something so different that we have no inkling what God would do with us. Rather, God may be perceived to be immanent in the world, and in this immanence to direct our course toward that which God could have us be. ("Immanence" is the usual term used to refer to the divine as existing within the universe as people may perceive it.) Because Christian teaching of divine transcendence is eschatological, it links this world with the world to come in the expectation and the experience of the believer.

Juridical Eschatology

Jesus' well-known parable of a feast to which the host makes surprising, insistent invitations—and equally categorical exclusions—voices another emphatic dimension of his own eschatology (see Matthew 22:1–14; Luke 14:16–24). God is portrayed as celebrating in God's kingdom with those who would join God, and as refusing to include those who have rejected the appointed way of entering the kingdom. Because Jesus was and is rightly known as the supreme teacher of divine love, this aspect of his teaching is frequently (and all too conveniently) ignored. But there is finally no compromise in love: it supersedes what would resist it. As the book of Psalms puts it, God's being king puts an end to everything wicked and those who represent wickedness, whether individuals or nations (see Psalm 10:15–16).

The lively sense of the judgment that is involved in God's final disclosure is a typical, sometimes a dominant, feature of Christianity. In this, Augustine of Hippo (354–430, discussed in *God,* an earlier volume in the Pilgrim Library of World Religions), delineates the sort of practice that would emerge during the Middle Ages. Speaking during the season of Lent, when the congregation prepares for the celebration of Easter and Christ's temptation in the wilderness is recalled, Augustine preached as follows (*Sermon* 206.1):

Life in this world is certainly the time of our humiliation. These days show—by the recurrence of this holy season—how the sufferings of the Lord Christ, who once suffered for us by death, are renewed each year. For what was done once and for all time so that our life might be renewed is solemnized each year so that the memory may be kept fresh. If, therefore, we ought to be humble of heart with sentiments of most sincere reverence throughout the entire period of our earthly sojourn when we live in the midst of temptations, how much more necessary is humility during these days, when we not only pass the time of our humiliation by living, but call attention to it by special devotion! The humility of Christ has taught us to be humble because he yielded to the wicked in his death; the exaltation of Christ lifts us up because by rising again he cleared the way for his devoted followers. Because, "if we have died with him, we shall also live with him; if we endure, we shall also reign with him" (2 Timothy 2:11–12). One of these conditions we now celebrate with due observance in view of his approaching passion; the other we shall celebrate after Easter when his Resurrection is, in like manner, accomplished again.

What Augustine is here signaling to us, in the clearest of terms, is the link between devotion to Christ and eschatology. Devotion to him (the imitation of Christ) is not merely encouraged because of Jesus' goodness, but because his life, death, and resurrection maps the path into God's kingdom. Jesus' example charts the single course for passing through the divine judgment which is necessarily a part of the coming of the kingdom.

Eschatological Conclusions

The three types of eschatology mentioned here are particularly mentioned because they correspond to major movements in the formative centuries of Christianity. Temporal eschatology typified the first two centuries; transcendent eschatology characterized the emergence of Christianity's philosophical dominance between the third century and the seventh century; juridical eschatology, of which Augustine is an early example, became the hallmark of Christianity from the Middle Ages onward. Although it may seem confusing to think of eschatology in these different ways, they are all a part of conceiving God as truly final. God's finality is such that God will definitively change not only time but also space and the nature of justice in human relations. Time and space and ethics are not totally different categories, but are essential dimensions of human experience, so eschatology rightly involves them all.[8]

Eschatology in all of its rich nuance constitutes the fundamental perspective from which Christianity addresses the problem of suffering. The God who makes the world also redeems the world, and God redeems the world we know, as it is. That may involve waiting over time (temporal eschatology), transforming the place where we stand (transcendent eschatology), and/or entering into a judgment that will change us (juridical eschatology), but in any and all cases, suffering is not the last word, but the transitional word before glory.

HOW IS SUFFERING REPRESENTED AND PERCEIVED AND EXPERIENCED?

Considerable space in this chapter has been devoted to the issues involved in understanding eschatology, because the type of eschatology Christianity embraces has determined its portrayal of the kind of pain that we encounter in our human suffering. That pain, in turn, relates to the anticipation of how God in Christ is to transform the world.

Temporal Eschatology: The Pain of Time

Once time is perceived as the principal dimension within which God acts definitively, the obvious question becomes, Just when will that be? We have already seen above that First Peter urges its readers to treat their current persecution as a "fiery ordeal," a test whose end would be glory for those who were proven (1 Peter 4:12–13). But how long was the ordeal to last? Does faith involve the simple assurance that in the end God will triumph, without knowledge of God's plan for God's people? Or does faith appropriately include a more precise insight into one's own redemption and the redemption of one's fellows? It is no coincidence that the letter called Second Peter addresses just these questions.

Second Peter is a work of the second century that is attributed to Peter, who probably died under Nero in Rome in 64 C.E. It follows the tradition of apocalyptic literature's being attributed to a great visionary from the past. (That tradition is also represented in the book of Daniel in the Old Testament and in Second Esdras in the Apocrypha.) Second Peter beautifully and classically sets out an account of how the pain of eschatological delay is experienced within apocalyptic Christianity, and how it might be addressed (2 Peter 3:1–10):

> This is already, beloved, a second letter I write to you; in them I arouse by reminder your sincere intent, to remember the sayings told in advance by the holy prophets and the commandment of your apostles of the Lord and Savior. First, know this: There will come at the last days scoffers with scoffing, going according to their own desires, and saying, Where is the promise of his coming?

Because although the patriarchs perished, everything remains the same from the beginning of creation!

This escapes those who like to think this way: Heavens existed from of old and earth subsisted from water and through water by the word of God. The world was then destroyed, deluged with water. But the present heavens and the earth by the same word are stored up for fire, kept for the day of judgment and the destruction of the godless. Do not let this one thing escape you, beloved: one day with the Lord is as a thousand years, and a thousand years as one day (Psalm 90:4). The Lord does not delay his promise, as some people suppose delay, but he is generous to you, not wishing you to be destroyed, but that all might attain to repentance.

The pain of time, that it remains unfulfilled by the presence of God, is dealt with by the understanding that it provides an interim for the purpose of repentance. That pain becomes an opportunity, to the extent that it is used as a preparation.

Transcendent Eschatology: The Pain of Place

Just as Origen believed that God through Christ had prepared "something more glorious and splendid than this present world," as we have seen, so he pondered what it means to conceive of God and of divine reward as beyond our ordinary terms of reference. His discussion appears within his use of the imagery of light to understand God (*On First Principles* 1.1.5):[9]

Having then refuted, to the best of our ability, every interpretation which suggests that we should attribute to God any material characteristics, we assert that he is in truth incomprehensible and immeasurable. For whatever may be the knowledge which we have been able to obtain about God, whether by perception or reflection, we must of necessity believe that he is far and away better than our thoughts about him. For if we see a man who can scarcely look at a glimmer of the light of the smallest lamp, and if we wish to teach such a one, whose eyesight is not strong enough to receive more light than we have said, about the brightness and splendor of the sun, shall we not have to tell him that the splendor of the sun is unspeakably and immeasurably better and more glorious than all this light he can see?

Here the imagery of pain is more than a matter of the discomfort one might feel in the ordinary course of living. The point is rather that our lives at their best do not prepare us to come in contact with God, and the little we know already is itself not something we can easily sustain. As in the myth of the cave in Plato's *Republic*, a person living in the dark will not readily be accustomed to light.

The difference between Origen and Plato is that, while in the myth of the cave the person can come into the sun's light, for Origen we cannot know God as God truly is in this life.[10] For that reason, pain is experienced in two directions at once. First, we are not naturally prepared to discover as much of God's light as we do, and that is a painful condition, as in Plato's myth. But second, we are also intrinsically unable to proceed from the intimations of God to the reality they point to, so that we cannot be completely fulfilled even after we have prepared ourselves for the light. So the pain of this life is both that it offers too much of the reality of God, and too little of it. The dilemma can only be resolved when we are in a difference place, when the transcendence of God, which presently impinges on our lives, becomes the whole of life as we know it. And because that can only occur beyond our world, present experience is not merely painful, but is itself a kind of pain.

Juridical Eschatology: The Pain of Self

In *Sermon* 205.1, preceding the sermon in which he explains the eschatological link between humility and exaltation, Augustine portrays the Christian life as inherently painful, and yet as in-

herently hopeful for that reason. What he says at the start of the
season of Lent is a classic exposition, which charts a course for
the development of spirituality during the Middle Ages:

> Today we commence the observance of Lent, the season now en-
> countering us in the course of the liturgical year. You are owed an
> appropriately solemn sermon, so that the word of God, brought
> to you through my ministry, may sustain you in spirit while you
> fast in body, and so that the inner man, thus refreshed by suitable
> food, may be able to accomplish and to persevere bravely in the
> disciplining of the outer man. For to my spirit of devotion it
> seems right that we, who are going to revere the Passion of our
> crucified Lord in the very near future, should construct for our-
> selves a cross of the bodily pleasures in need of restraint, as the
> Apostle says, "And they who belong to Christ have crucified their
> flesh with its passions and desires" (Galatians 5:24).

Pain here is actually a gate to the promise of transformation.
The fact of our selfish desires, which we experience in our flesh,
is what keeps us from appreciating and joining ourselves to the
love of God, in Augustine's thought (see especially his magiste-
rial work, *The City of God*).[11] So the willing experience of pain
actually permits us to know our true selves, to make a cross
from what alienates us from God, and so through the death of
selfishness to understand who we truly are before God.

Juridical eschatology is the source of Christianity's profound
skepticism about the value of human life in the flesh. The problem is not so much the material of which we are made, as what
has become of it by means of human selfishness. Indulgence of
the flesh is where we try to make gods of ourselves, and in so
doing dishonor each other in our abuse of passion as much as
we dishonor God. For Augustine, war, crime, exploitation, and
the violent results of all three are not happenstances. When he

learns of such things, the news does not come to him as a sudden realization that life as we know it (in the flesh) is beset by evil. Rather, he recognizes that these evils must be overcome by a recognition of our truer selves, selves not subservient to that selfishness.

WHY DOES SUFFERING MATTER, AND HOW DO WE DEAL WITH, OR OVERCOME, SUFFERING?

Evil comes to Christianity, then, in distinct ways. There is the suffering of time, the suffering of place, the suffering of self. Temporal eschatology longs for a different time, transcendent eschatology for a difference place, juridical eschatology for a different self. (What is striking is that these anxieties—of time, place, and self—are precisely the most persistent troubles of modernity. But where eschatology offers a prospect of resolution, secular therapies can give only assuagement.) Yet just where one might expect that these distinct kinds of suffering would develop into distinct responses, Christianity in fact teaches a single, unambiguous strategy, grounded in the teaching of Jesus.

In *Sacred Texts and Authority*, we have already called attention to the theology of Martin Luther King Jr. in his "Letter from Birmingham Jail." There, he set out the fundamental position behind his teaching of nonviolence:

> One has not only a legal but a moral responsibility to obey just laws. Conversely, one has a moral responsibility to disobey unjust laws. I would agree with St. Augustine that "an unjust law is no law at all."

Brave and lucid though that policy is, it is grounded in the more radical teaching of Jesus, perhaps best expressed in the following advice (Matthew 5:38–42):

You have heard that it was said, An eye for an eye and a tooth for a tooth. Yet I say to you not to resist the evil one. But to someone who strikes you on the right cheek, turn also the other. And to one who wants to enter judgment with you to take your tunic, give your garment, too! And with someone who compels a mile's journey from you, travel with him two. Give to the one who asks of you, and do not turn away from one who wants to borrow from you.

Of all the teachings of Jesus, none is more straightforward, and none more challenging. Evil is to be overcome by means of what is usually called nonresistance.

What follows in Matthew states the principle of Jesus' teaching, that we are to love in the way that God does (Matthew 5:43–48; see Luke 6:36). The fundamental quality of that teaching within Christianity is unquestionable (see Matthew 22:34–40; Mark 12:28–34; Luke 10:25–28; Romans 13:8–10). Yet in the teaching about turning the other cheek, giving the garment, going the extra mile, offering the money, everything comes down to particular conditions that prevailed during the Roman occupation of the Near East. The fact that this formulation only appears in Matthew (written around 80 C.E.) has given rise to the legitimate question whether it should be attributed to Jesus in its present form. The imagery corresponds to the conditions of the Roman occupation in an urban area, where a soldier of the empire might well demand provisions and service and money, and all with the threat of force. But even if we acknowledge (as seems only reasonable) that Matthew's Gospel has pitched Jesus' policy in the idiom of its own experience, the policy itself should be attributed to Jesus.

Why should what is usually called nonresistance to evil be recommended? It needs to be stressed that nonresistance is not the same as acquiescence. The injustice that is done is never accepted as if it were just. The acts of turning the other cheek, giving the garment, going the additional mile, offering the money, are all are designed to be excessive, so that the fact of the injustice of what is demanded is underlined. Indeed, it is not really accurate to call the behavior "nonresistance." The point is for the person who makes demands that are unjust to realize they are unjust. Just that policy served Christians and their faith well during the centuries of persecution under the Roman Empire. It was effective because it brought about an awareness within the empire, even among the enemies of Christianity, that the policy of violent persecution was unjust (and, for that matter, ineffective). Rather than a teaching of nonresistance, this is a version of the advice of how to retaliate. Instead of an eye for an eye, it suggests a cheek after a cheek. This is not non-resistance; it is exemplary response. That is, it is a form of retal-iation: not to harm, but to show another way.

The hope that the other way—God's way—will be seen by means of exemplary response, and that once it has been seen it will be followed, is basic to Jesus' policy of exemplary response. That hope is articulated by the three types of eschatology we have seen, in each of which God's ultimate vindication is what awaits the believer at the end. But in every case (as we will go on now to see), the same basic policy of exemplary response is urged as the only authentically Christian response to suffering in the present.

Just after 1 Peter 4:12–14 (cited above) refers to the promise involved in sharing Christ's sufferings, the letter spells out its own advice of exemplary response (1 Peter 4:14–19):

> If you are reviled for the name of Christ, you are blessed, because the spirit of glory—even God's own spirit—rests upon you. Be-cause none of you is to suffer as a murderer or thief or doer of bad or meddler: but if as a Christian, let him not be ashamed, but give glory to God by this name. Because now is time for judgment to begin with the house of God; and if first with us, what will the end

be of those who disobey the gospel of God? And if the just person is barely saved, where shall the irreverent and the sinful appear? So let those who suffer according to the will of God commend their lives to a faithful creator in doing good.

The reality of suffering is not only acknowledged, but celebrated, because the pain of the present time, a function of the injustice of the world, is transitional to the glory that is to come. The only real danger, within this temporal eschatology, is that Christians might begin to commit injustice, since they are treated as criminals in any case. The letter addresses just that worry, while it firmly articulates a classic response to the reality of unjustly suffering pain.

So classic is this expression of the Christian response to suffering and pain that we find it incorporated within the other two distinct eschatologies already described. Origen, in *On First Principles*, provides insight into how a transcendent eschatology may take up the imperative of exemplary response. For Origen, the source of suffering is not physical pain as such. That may seem ironic, since he without question experienced the most torture of all the theologians mentioned here. But Origen's was no merely personal theology. To his mind, our actual source of pain is what occurs within our own passions and desires when they are disordered so as not to prepare themselves for the knowledge of God. Yet Origen is also categorical in insisting that Christianity is not about the denial of passion or desire as such (*On First Principles* 3.2.2):

Are we to think that the devil is the cause of our being hungry or thirsty? I guess there is no one who would venture to maintain such a thing. If then he is not the cause of our being hungry or thirsty, what of that time when an individual has reached the age of puberty and this involves the arousal of natural desire? It fol-

lows without a doubt that, as the devil is not the cause of our being hungry or thirsty, so neither is he the cause of that impulse
which is naturally present at maturity, the desire for sexual intercourse. It is certain that this impulse is by no means always incited
by the devil, so as to lead us to think that if there were no devil our
bodies would not have the wish for such intercourse.

This unusually blunt statement makes it clear that, for Origen,
the problem of the evil people do cannot be pawned off on the
flesh or the devil. The source of evil is rather what we do with
our natural (and naturally good) desires.

That is what leads Origen to the conclusion that we must
treat our own desires as Matthew's Jesus would have us treat
Roman soldiers: with an exemplary response (*On First Principles* 3.2.4):

> We must bear in mind, all the while, that nothing more happens
> to us as a result of good or evil thoughts which are suggested to
> our heart, but a simple agitation and excitement which urges us
> on to deeds of good or evil. It is possible for us, when an evil
> power has begun to urge us on to a deed of evil, to dismiss the evil
> suggestion and to resist the mean enticement, and to do nothing
> at all worthy of blame. And it is possible on the other hand when
> a divine power has urged us on to better things, not to follow its
> guidance, since our capacity of free will is maintained for us in ei-
> ther case.

Even a suggestion to do injustice need not be enacted along the
lines of its evil intent, but may be followed and pursued to
the extent it shows passion for what is good. Origen, one of the
greatest teachers of spirituality, shows us how the rule of exemplary response may be followed within our hearts, to nurture
our passions toward the transcendent vision of God.

Now as it happens, Augustine—in quite a different analysis of hunger and thirst—offers an alternative for understanding pain (*Sermon* 240.3):

> Now if I said that the body would rise again to be hungry and thirsty, to be sick and suffer, to be subject to decay, you would rightly refuse to believe me. True, the flesh now suffers these needs and afflictions. Why? Sin is the cause. We have all sinned in one man [Augustine refers here to Adam], and we have all been born into corruption. Sin is the cause of all our evils. In fact, it is not without reason that people suffer all these evils. God is just; God is omnipotent. We would not suffer these evils in any way if we did not deserve them. But since we were subjected to these punishments to which we are obliged because of our sins, our Lord Jesus Christ wished to partake of our punishments without any guilt on his part. By enduring the penalty without any guilt, he cancelled both the guilt and the penalty. He cancelled the guilt by forgiving sins, the penalty, by rising from the dead. He promised this and he wished us to walk in hope. Let us persevere, and we will come to the reward.

With extraordinary clarity, Augustine sets out the juridical eschatology that would be a controlling influence in the West during the Middle Ages and the Reformation. Pain is now something that we accept with an exemplary response, which itself takes up the model of Jesus Christ. Suffering patiently brings the reward that has been made possible because of the single one who suffered innocently. The humanity that was lost in the case of Adam is more than recovered in the case of Christ.

SUFFERING AND EVIL: THE LARGER QUESTION OF ETIOLOGY AND THEODICY

If you want to start an argument among believing Christians, ask the following question: Does the devil really exist?

No creed actually settles that question, although some Christians insist that belief in Satan is a litmus test of true faith, while others see Satan as a personification of human evil. Biblical usage does not resolve the question, either, since Satan's role begins as an accuser within the *heavenly* court (Job 1:6) and ends when he is tormented for his rebellion in a lake of fire (Revelation 20:7–10).[12]

That image in the Revelation of John is representative of what temporal eschatology makes of Satan. He deceives and oppresses the people of God in the present; as First Peter puts it (5:8–9):

> Be sober, be alert. Your opponent the devil like a roaring lion walks around, seeking to devour. Resist him, steadfast in the faith, knowing that the same sort of sufferings are completed in the world by your brotherhood.

But because the whole point of this adversary's power is that it is provisional and limited (whatever its claims for itself or appearances might be), apocalyptic thought clearly portrays Satan as a subservient figure. His reality is that he is in charge of an order that is passing away, and that he is increasingly violent in his own passing into oblivion.

But is this oblivion a nothingness, or should we imagine Satan as eternally punished? That is the question that the argument about Satan naturally leads to, and it is the crux of the matter in theological terms. At just this point, Origen and Augustine go their separate and distinct ways. And their disagreement is emblematic of the genuine controversy, in profoundly theological terms, that is going on within Christianity at the moment.

Killed during the persecution of one emperor, centuries after his death, Origen was condemned by another emperor, Justinian I (in an edict of 543).[13] That condemnation marks the growing influence of Augustinianism, and the increasing embarrassment about Origen over the centuries that followed his death. Among those embarrassments was Origen's teaching that the restoration of all things in Christ would include the salvation of the devil and his angels.[14] Origen's commitment to transcendent eschatology was such that he envisaged the entire realm of creation, seen and unseen, as transformed by means of the love of Christ. Evidently, the devil for him was real in the world of temptations (as we have already seen), but insubstantial as compared to the power of God.

Augustine, on the other hand, was equally committed to a juridical eschatology. The triumph of Christ necessarily involves the defeat of Satan, and that means his defeat is implicitly permanent (*Sermon* 263.1):

> The devil exulted when Christ died, and by that very death of Christ the devil was overcome. In a way, he took food from a trap. He gloated over the death as if he had been appointed a delegate of death. What he rejoiced in became a prison for him. The cross of the Lord became a trap for the devil. The death of the Lord was the food by which he was ensnared.

This powerful rhetoric is effective in two ways. First, as has already been suggested, it makes Satan a figure of necessarily permanent opposition to Christ. The synods that condemned Origen posthumously were a posthumous triumph for Augustine. Second, it makes the devil himself the victim of the kind of temptation that he represents: temptation is marked out as the principal enemy of the Christian, in a way that set the stage for the spirituality of the Middle Ages. Every sin must be paid for, and therefore Satan must constantly pay.

CONCLUSION

Christianity is committed irrevocably to the goodness of what God created. It is realistic about acknowledging—and even emphasizing—the pain and the suffering involved in being human. The resolution between divine goodness and our suffering is found in the teaching of eschatology: God is transforming our world to make us participants in God's glory. That transformation is sometimes conceived of as happening more over time (temporal eschatology), sometimes more through the space that God creates anew (transcendent eschatology), sometimes more by the purification of our moral natures (juridical eschatology). But Christians are in agreement that it is our exemplary response to evil, after the pattern of Jesus, that permits us access to God's living transformation. That emphasis is so all-consuming that the issue of whether God's adversary and ours, Satan, can be said to exist in the way God does remains a matter of debate, and a secondary concern.

CHAPTER 4

Judaism

WHY ARE EVIL, SUFFERING, AND PAIN
A PROBLEM FOR JUDAISM?

A monotheist religion faces a critical challenge in dealing with evil, suffering, and pain. That is because such a religion holds that God is both all-powerful and good. But then why does God, who is good, permit or even bring about suffering?[1] If it is meant as punishment, then why do the good suffer and the evil prosper? That question attests to the character of monotheist faith that the one and only God who made heaven and earth governs the world and carries out God's will through what happens in the world. Judaism for its part finds it necessary to explain the existence of evil, suffering, and pain. A just God cannot act unjustly. So Abraham said to God in pleading for the lives of the people of Sodom: "Will you sweep away the innocent along with the guilty? Far be it from you to do such a thing, to bring death upon the innocent as well as the guilty, so that innocent and guilty fare alike. Far be it from you! Shall not the Judge of all the earth deal justly?" (Genesis 18:25).

If God makes peace and creates evil as much as good, and if God is responsible for all that happens, including these things, then God does the bad as much as the good things that happen to us. And that raises, for Judaism, the problem of evil, for evil in the world requires an explanation: how can God, who is good and also all-powerful, permit it? Suffering must express God's will, and therefore requires an explanation. Pain, individual and collective, also has to mean something and cannot happen accidentally. And, finally and most important, why bad things happen to good people demands an explanation. All together, therefore, suffering and pain present challenges to the Judaic theologians in the classic Torah, written and oral.

The other monotheist religions address the same problem of evil in the same terms. But Judaism meets a further problem of its own: evil, suffering, and pain touch not only the individual but the entire holy community, and the fate of Israel, that community of the elect, cannot be distinguished from the fate of the Israelite individual man or woman. So the problem of evil shades over into the issue of Israel's fate in history, and when we recall that by "Israel" Judaism means the people of God, whom God first loved, and not a merely secular ethnic group, the theological challenge from evil done through history to holy Israel joins the problem of evil formulated in personal and individual terms. The nature of the problem becomes clear when we recall that, in Judaism, the same word is used for the private person and the entire religious community. That word is "Israel," and it stands for the holy community as a whole, but may also refer to an individual member of that same community, that is, an Israelite (in secular language, a Jew).

Judaism, as a monotheist religion, could not resort to the explanation that an evil God brought evil, a good God, good. Nor could Judaism concede that God did not have the power to prevent evil and suffering. Time and again, in Scripture, Israel appeals to God to save the people "for the sake of your Name," meaning, "lest the gentiles say, 'Where is their God?' Or, 'Their God has no power.'" And while suffering as retribution for sin would play a large role in Judaic explanations of evil, the challenge of why the wicked prosper, raised by Jeremiah and fully exposed in the book of Job, would never produce an easy response.

But that is not to suggest that the Judaic classics provide no answers at all. Perhaps the single paramount one is the conception that suffering punishes sin—but also atones for sin. That conception comes to expression in many forms, but there is a very particular one. Let me explain the text we are about to consider. It is in two parts, a citation of statements at tractate Abot ("the Fathers") 5:8–9, and an amplification of those same statements in *The Fathers according to Rabbi Nathan.*

> There are seven forms of punishment which come upon the world for seven kinds of transgression. (1) [If] some people give tithes and some people do not give tithes, there is a famine from drought.
>
> If some people do, and some people do not, set aside the portion for the priestly ration, a famine because of tumult comes upon the world.
>
> If some people do, and some do not set aside dough-offering, there is a famine of annihilation that comes upon the world.
>
> [If] everyone decided not to tithe, the heavens will be closed up so as not to yield dew and rain, and people will labor but not suffice.
>
> The specification of punishment for particular sins or transgressions means to underscore the appropriate character of the penalty, which fits the crime.
>
> R. Josiah says, "On account of the sin of neglecting the dough offering, a blessing does not come upon the produce, so that people labor but do not suffice.
>
> "On account of the sin of neglecting the separation of a portion of the crop for the priestly ration and the separation of tithes, the heavens will be closed up so as not to yield dew and rain, and people will be handed over to the government [to be sold into slavery for non-payment of their taxes in kind]."
>
> Pestilence comes to the world on account of neglect of the

requirement to leave in the fields the defective grape, the forgotten sheaf, and the corner of the field, as well as to separate tithe for the poor person.

Now we are given a concrete story of how people suffer because of failure to leave enough food for the poor, such as the requirement to leave defective grapes, sheaves, and the corner of the field ought to provide. The reason for pestilence in particular is spelled out:

> There is the case of a woman who lived in the neighborhood of a landlord, and her two sons went out to gather [the crops that are to be left for the poor], but did not find any produce in the field.
>
> Their mother said, "When my sons come from the field, perhaps I'll find something in their hands to eat."
>
> For their part, they were saying, "When we get home, perhaps we'll find something in mother's hands to eat."
>
> She found nothing with them, nor they with her, to eat. They put their heads on their mother's lap and all three of them died on one day.
>
> The Holy One, blessed be he, said to them, "You people have exacted from them their lives! By your lives! I shall exact from you your lives."
>
> And so Scripture says, *Do not rob from the weak, because he is weak, nor crush the poor in the gate, for the Lord will plead their cause and take the life of those who despoil them* (Proverbs 22:22–23).

Now we move from individual to collective, social sins:

> A sword comes into the world because of the delaying of justice and perversion of justice, and because of those who teach the Torah not in accord with the law.

The story of sages, public figures, now amplifies the failures of those who do not teach the Torah properly:

> When they seized Rabban Simeon b. Gamaliel and R. Ishmael on the count of death, Rabban Simeon b. Gamaliel was in session and was perplexed, saying, "Woe is us! For we are put to death like those who profane the Sabbath and worship idols and practice fornication and kill."
>
> Said to him R. Ishmael b. Elisha, "Would it please you if I said something before you?"
>
> He said to him, "Go ahead."
>
> He said to him, "Is it possible that when you were sitting at a banquet, poor folk came and stood at your door, and you did not let them come in and eat?"
>
> He said to him, "By heaven [may I be cursed] if I ever did such a thing! Rather, I set up guards at the gate. When poor folk came along, they would bring them in to me and eat and drink with me and say a blessing for the sake of Heaven."
>
> He said to him, "Is it possible that when you were in session and expounding [the Torah] on the Temple mount and the vast populations of Israelites were in session before you, you took pride in yourself?"
>
> He said to him, "Ishmael my brother, one has to be ready to accept his failing. [That is why I am being put to death, the pride that I felt on such an occasion.]"
>
> They went on appealing to the executioner for grace. This one [Ishmael] said to him, "I am a priest, son of a high priest, kill me first, so that I do not have to witness the death of my companion."
>
> And the other [Simeon] said, "I am the patriarch, son of the patriarch, kill me first, so that I do not have to witness the death of my companion."
>
> He said to him, "Cast lots." They cast lots, and the lot fell on Rabban Simeon b. Gamaliel.

The executioner took the sword and cut off his head.

R. Ishmael b. Elisha took it and held it in his breast and wept and cried out: "O holy mouth, O faithful mouth, O mouth that brought forth beautiful gems, precious stones and pearls! Who has laid you in the dust, who has filled your mouth with dirt and dust.

"Concerning you Scripture says, *Awake, O sword, against my shepherd and against the man who is near to me* (Zechariah 13:7)."

He had not finished speaking before the executioner took the sword and cut off his head.

Concerning them Scripture says, *My wrath shall wax hot, and I will kill you with the sword, and your wives shall be widows, and your children fatherless* (Exodus 22:23).

To understand the next cause of suffering, we have to keep in mind that, for holy Israel, exile from the Holy Land brings about much anguish. The original exile, in 586 B.C.E., was brought about, the Scriptures made clear, by reason of sin; Israel then went to exile in Babylonia, and hence moving from one country to another—specifically, the promised land to any other—was deemed suffering on account of sin. Now the oral Torah's sages tell us what sins in particular:

Exile comes into the world because of those who worship idols, because of fornication, and because of bloodshed, and because of the neglect of the release of the Land [in the year of release].

On account of idolatry, as it is said: *And I will destroy your high places . . . and I will scatter you among the nations* (Leviticus 26:30, 33).

Said the Holy One, blessed be he, to Israel, "Since you lust after idolatry, so I shall send you into exile to a place in which there is idolatry.

Therefore it is said, *And I will destroy your high places . . . and I will scatter you among the nations.*

Because of fornication: Said R. Ishmael b. R. Yosé, "So long as the Israelites are lawless in fornication, the Presence of God takes its leave of them," as it is said, *That he not see an unseemly thing in you and turn away from you* (Deuteronomy 23:15).

Because of bloodshed: *So you shall not pollute the land in which you are located, for blood pollutes the land* (Numbers 35:33).

Because of neglect of the release of the Land in the year of release: how do we know that that is the case?

Then shall the land be paid her Sabbaths (Leviticus 26:34).

Said the Holy One, blessed be he, to Israel, "Since you do not propose to give the land its rest, it will give you a rest. For the number of months that you did not give the land rest, it will take a rest on its own.

That is why it is said, *Even then shall the land rest and repay her Sabbaths, as long as it lies desolate it shall have rest, even the rest that it did not have on your Sabbaths, when you lived on it* (Leviticus 26:35).

— *The Fathers according to Rabbi Nathan,* chapter 38

When we take a second look at this systematic exposition, we come to a clearer picture of why suffering and evil form a problem for Judaism. The Scriptures explicitly tied Israelite suffering to God's plan. They account for individual suffering by appeal to divine decree—Eve is told in so many words, for example, that on account of the sin of disobedience, she would bear children in pain (Genesis 3:16). But, in context of greater weight, the fate of the entire holy people bears witness to its moral condition. Hence, so far as Judaism proposed to account for the long and sometimes sorry history of the Jews as a group, treating that group as the "Israel" of which Scripture speaks, Judaism would have to address each occasion of suffering and disaster and turn them all into moments of renewal. So the prayer of the synagogue on the Sabbath would state: "On account of our sins we are exiled from our land," and in this and many other expressions, Judaism acknowledges its task of explaining, but not explaining away, suffering and evil in the world.

HOW IS SUFFERING REPRESENTED AND PERCEIVED AND EXPERIENCED?

Suffering as a mode of atonement for sin frames the principal representation of the matter in the Pentateuchal writings, both in Leviticus 26 and Deuteronomy 34. If Israel does not obey, "I will wreak misery upon you, consumption and fever, which cause the eyes to pine and the body to languish. . . . And if for all that you do not obey me, I will make your skies like iron and your earth like copper . . . your land shall not yield its produce" (Leviticus 26:16–22). These modes of local suffering moreover find their match in the fate of the holy people: "You shall be routed by your enemies, and your foes shall dominate you." The source of suffering then is in Israel's own disobedience to the covenant that it has made with God, and that comes about by reason of rebellion, the people's arrogantly following their will, not God's. Numerous examples of how God metes out justice in exact measure are set forth in Scripture and tallied by the oral Torah as well. For example, in the following, the pain and suffering of Samson, Absalom, the honor paid to Miriam, Joseph, and Moses, all form expressions of God's exact justice:

> Samson followed his eyes [where they led him], therefore the Philistines put out his eyes, since it is said, And the Philistines laid hold on him and put out his eyes (Judges 16:21).
> Absalom was proud of his hair, therefore he was hung by his hair (2 Samuel 14:25–26). And since he had sexual relations with ten concubines of his father, therefore they thrust ten

spear heads into his body, since it is said, And ten young men that carried Jacob's armor surrounded and smote Absalom and killed him (2 Samuel 18:15).

And since he stole three hearts—his father's, the court's, and the Israelite's—since it is said, And Absalom stole the heart of the men of Israel (2 Samuel 15:6)—therefore three darts were thrust into him, since it is said, And he took three darts in his hand and thrust them through the heart of Absalom (2 Samuel 18:14).

—Mishnah-tractate Sotah 1:8

And so is it on the good side:

Miriam waited a while for Moses, since it is said, And his sister stood afar off (Exodus 2:4), therefore, Israel waited on her seven days in the wilderness, since it is said, And the people did not travel on until Miriam was brought in again (Numbers 12:15).

Joseph had the merit of burying his father, and none of his brothers was greater than he, since it is said, And Joseph went up to bury his father . . . and there went up with him both chariots and horsemen (Genesis 50:7, 9).

We have none so great as Joseph, for only Moses took care of his [bones].

Moses had the merit of burying the bones of Joseph, and none in Israel was greater than he, since it is said, And Moses took the bones of Joseph with him (Exodus 13:19).

We have none so great as Moses, for only the Holy One, blessed be he, took care of his [bones], since it is said, "And he buried him in the valley" (Deuteronomy 34:6).

And not of Moses alone have they stated [this rule], but of all righteous people, since it is said, And your righteousness shall go before you. The glory of the Lord shall gather you [in death] (Isaiah 58:8).

—Mishnah-tractate Sotah 1:9

We see, therefore, that divine justice requires the suffering of the wicked. Suffering then represents retribution for sin.

It goes without saying that the fate of the holy people corresponds to the condition of the faith of the people. When Israel obeys, it prospers; when not, it suffers. In many ways Israel embodies in the Holy Land the fate of Adam in the Garden of Eden. Suffering is built into the human condition, because humanity has fallen from Eden, by reason of its own actions, and brought about its present circumstance. It is normal for humanity to suffer, just as God had meant the normal situation of humanity to be Paradise, just as the normal situation of holy Israel was to be the Land of Israel, the promised land. Neither worked out. First comes Adam and Eve, suffering exile from Eden by reason of sin:

> R. Abbahu in the name of R. Yosé bar Haninah: "It is written, 'But they are like a man [Adam], they have transgressed the covenant' (Hosea 6:7).
>
> "'They are like a man,' specifically, like the first man. [We shall now compare the story of the first man in Eden with the story of Israel in its land.]
>
> "'In the case of the first man, I brought him into the garden of Eden, I commanded him, he violated my commandment, I judged him to be sent away and driven out, but I mourned for him, saying "How . . ." [which begins the book of Lamentations, hence stands for a lament, but which, as we just saw, also is written with the consonants that also yield, 'Where are you'].
>
> "'I brought him into the garden of Eden,' as it is written, 'And the Lord God took the man and put him into the garden of Eden' (Gen. 2:15).
>
> "'I commanded him,' as it is written, 'And the Lord God commanded . . .' (Genesis 2:16).
>
> "'And he violated my commandment,' as it is written, 'Did

you eat from the tree concerning which I commanded you'
(Genesis 3:11).

"'I judged him to be sent away,' as it is written, 'And the
Lord God sent him from the garden of Eden' (Genesis 3:23).

"'And I judged him to be driven out.' 'And he drove out the
man' (Genesis 3:24).

"'But I mourned for him, saying, "How . . ."' 'And he said
to him, "Where are you"' (Genesis 3:9), and the word for
'where are you' is written, 'How . . .'

"'So too in the case of his descendants, [God continues to
speak,] I brought them into the Land of Israel, I commanded
them, they violated my commandment, I judged them to be
sent out and driven away but I mourned for them, saying,
"How . . ."'

"'I brought them into the Land of Israel.' 'And I brought
you into the land of Carmel' (Jeremiah 2:7).

"'I commanded them.' 'And you, command the children
of Israel' (Exodus 27:20). 'Command the children of Israel'
(Leviticus 24:2).

"'They violated my commandment.' 'And all Israel have
violated your Torah' (Daniel 9:11).

"'I judged them to be sent out.' 'Send them away, out of
my sight and let them go forth' (Jeremiah 15:1).

"'. . . and driven away.' 'From my house I shall drive them'
(Hosea 9:15).

"'But I mourned for them, saying, "How . . ."' 'How has the
city sat solitary, that was full of people' (Lamentations 1:1)."

—Genesis Rabbah XIX:IX

Not only so, but the history of Israel, portrayed from Genesis through Kings—that is, from creation to the destruction of
the Temple and the exile from the Holy Land—acts out in vast
detail the story of the fall of Adam and Eve from grace. That
was through their own doing, their act of disobedience, and the
same was so of Israel. That same representation of Israel's suffer-

ing as a reflex of Israel's arrogance and disobedience accounts, also, for the advent of the false messiah, Bar Kokhba, not a mythic but a historical figure of the early second century c.e. But in the oral Torah, Bar Kokhba is portrayed as false, specifically because of the sin of arrogance against God, and that is what accounts for the defeat of Israel in its struggle with Rome of that period: When Ben Koziba would go forth to battle, he would say, "Lord of the world! Do not help and do not hinder us! 'Hast thou not rejected us, O God? Thou dost not go forth, O God, with our armies'" (Psalms 60:10).

Three and a half years did Hadrian besiege Betar.

R. Eleazar of Modiin would sit on sack cloth and ashes and pray every day, saying "Lord of the worlds! Do not sit in judgment today! Do not sit in judgment today!"

Hadrian wanted to go to him. A Samaritan said to him, "Do not go to him until I see what he is doing, and so hand over the city [of Betar] to you. ['Make peace . . . for you.']"

He got into the city through a drain pipe. He went and found R. Eleazar of Modiin standing and praying. He pretended to whisper something into his ear.

The townspeople saw him do this and brought him to Ben Kozeba. They told him, "We saw this man having dealings with your uncle."

He said to him, 'What did you say to him, and what did he say to you?"

He said to him, "If I tell you, then the king will kill me, and if I do not tell you, then you will kill me. It is better that the king kill me and not you."

He said to him, "He said to me, 'I shall hand over my city.' ['I shall make peace. . . .']"

He went to R. Eleazar of Modiin. He said to him, "What did this Samaritan say to you?"

He replied, "Nothing."

He said to him, "What did you say to him?"

He said to him, "Nothing."

[Ben Kozeba] gave [Eleazar] one good kick and killed him.
Forthwith an echo came forth and proclaimed the following
verse:

"Woe to my worthless shepherd, who deserts the flock! May
the sword smite his arm and his right eye! Let his arm be wholly
withered, his right eye utterly blinded!" (Zechariah 11:17).

"You have murdered Eleazar of Modiin, the arm of all Israel and their right eye. Therefore may the right arm of that
man wither, may his right eye be utterly blinded!"

Forthwith Betar was taken, and Ben Kozeba was killed.

— Palestinian Talmud Tractate Taanit 4:5/VII.[1]

The arrogance of Ben Koziba, expressed both in what he said to
God and also in his treatment of the sainted sage, accounts for
the suffering of that occasion. The Messiah will be known for
humility, not pride, in the Judaic religion.[2]

So much for the suffering of the holy people. What about
our own suffering, and how do we deal with death? Here, sages
take a view consistent with their notion of God's perfect goodness, so death is not a form of suffering at all:

In the Torah belonging to R. Meir people found written, "And behold, it was very good" (Genesis 1:31) [means] "And behold, death
is good." [The play is on the word "very," M'D, and "death,"
MWT.]

Said R. Samuel bar Nahman, "I was riding on my grandfather's
shoulder, going up from my town to Kefar Hana through Bet
Shean, and I heard R. Simeon b. R. Eleazar in session and ex-
pounding in the name of R. Meir, "'And behold, it was very
good'—'And behold, death is good.'"

Hama bar Hanina and R. Jonathan conducted the following
argument:

Hama bar Hanina said, "The first man was worthy not to have to taste the taste of death. And why was the penalty of death applied to him? The Holy One, blessed be he, foresaw that Nebuchadnezzar and Hiram were destined to turn themselves into gods. Therefore the penalty of having to die was imposed upon man. That is in line with this verse of Scripture: 'You were in Eden, the garden of God' (Ezekiel 28:13). And was Hiram actually in Eden? But he said to him, 'You are the one who caused that one in Eden to have to die.'"

Said R. Jonathan to him, "If so, God should have decreed death only for the wicked, but not for the righteous. Rather, it was so that the wicked should not be able hypocritically to pretend to repent, so that they should not have occasion to say, 'Are not the righteous living on and on? It is only because they form a treasure of merit accruing on account of the practice of doing religious duties as well as good deeds. We too shall lay up a treasure of merit accruing from doing religious duties and good deeds.' What would come out is that the things they do would not be done sincerely, [for their own sake, but only for the sake of gaining merit]. [That is what is good about death. It prevents the wicked from perverting the holy life by doing the right thing for the wrong reason. Everyone dies, so there is no point in doing religious duties only so as to avoid dying.]"

Here the same question is raised by other sages:

R. Yohanan and R. Simeon b. Laqish:
Yohanan said, "On what account was a decree of death issued against the wicked? It is because, so long as the wicked live, they anger the Holy One, blessed be he. That is in line with the following verse of Scripture: 'You have wearied the Lord with your deeds' (Malachi 2:17). When they die, they stop angering the Holy One, blessed be he. That is in line with the following verse of Scripture: 'There the wicked cease from rag-

ing' (Job 3:17). There the wicked cease angering the Holy One, blessed be he.

"On what account, however, is the decree of death issued against the righteous? It is because so long as the righteous live, they have to conduct warfare against their impulse to do evil. When they die, they find rest. That is in line with this verse: 'And there the weary are at rest' (Job 3:17). 'It is enough, we have labored long enough.'"

Simeon b. Laqish said, "It is so as to give an ample reward for the one, and to exact ample punishment from the other. To give ample reward to the righteous, who really never were worthy of having to taste the taste of death but accepted the taste of death for themselves. Therefore: 'in their land they shall possess double' (Isaiah 61:7).

"'And to exact ample punishment from the wicked,' for the righteous had not been worthy of having to taste the taste of death but they had accepted the taste of death for themselves on account [of the wicked]. Therefore: 'And destroy them with a double destruction' (Jeremiah 17:18)."

—Genesis Rabbah IX:V.1–3

The premise of all the passages we have considered is the same: God is just, and when we suffer, we have to seek an explanation in rational terms. We shall find a reason, even though it is not our reason, for all that happens. And therein lies the extraordinary dilemma that evil and suffering present to the monotheist religions in general, and to Judaism in particular.

WHY DOES SUFFERING MATTER, AND HOW DO WE DEAL WITH, OR OVERCOME, SUFFERING?

We deal with suffering through atonement, and we accept suffering as divine punishment. That principle governs both individual and communal life. It is expressed first by Amos,[3]

when he says, "You alone have I singled out of all the families of
the earth, that is why I will visit upon you all your iniquities"
(Amos 3:2). This conception builds upon the foregoing and
makes Israel's suffering a mark of divine love. That accounts,
also, for the suffering of the Messiah at Isaiah 53:3ff.: "He was
wounded because of our sins, crushed because of our iniquities." In the oral Torah, the counterpart representation of suffering takes the form of "suffering inflicted out of divine love." It
is regarded as a privilege to suffer, since in this world one
thereby atones for sins, making certain one's entry into the
world to come.[4] The conception, a key to the Judaic presenta-
tion of suffering, deserves ample consideration, because it is not
entirely familiar in the repertoire of religious interpretation of
the evil that comes upon us.

The proper way to deal with suffering then is, in the language of the oral Torah (Babylonian Talmud tractate Berakhot
5a), "If a person sees that sufferings afflict him, let him examine
his deeds." The full exposition of how the oral Torah portrays
the proper response to suffering shows us, in concrete detail,
precisely the way in which suffering is made to matter. It is not
explained away but explained as critical to God's purpose and
central in God's showing love for us. The passage, at Babylonian Talmud tractate Berakhot 5a–b/III.10–21, follows:

> Said Raba, and some say, R. Hisda, "If a person sees that sufferings
> afflict him, let him examine his deeds.
>
> "For it is said, 'Let us search and try our ways and return to the
> Lord' (Lamentations 3:40).
>
> "If he examined his ways and found no cause [for his suffer-
> ing], let him blame the matter on his wasting [time better spent in
> studying] the Torah.
>
> "For it is said, 'Happy is the man whom you chastise, O Lord,
> and teach out of your Torah' (Psalms 94:12).

"If he blamed it on something and found [after correcting the fault] that that had not, in fact, been the cause at all, he may be sure that he suffers the afflictions that come from God's love.

"For it is said, 'For the one whom the Lord loves he corrects' (Proverbs 3:12)."

The premise of the opening proposition is that our own deeds bring about suffering, and various causes for suffering are to be identified. The correct attitude for suffering is thankfulness: "Happy is the man whom you chastise." But if, in sin, we find no clear cause, then it comes about through God's love, and this is the meaning of "suffering by reason of God's love." The passage now spells out precisely what this means:

Said Raba said R. Sehorah said R. Huna [said], "Whomever the Holy One, blessed be he, prefers he crushes with suffering.

"For it is said, 'The Lord was pleased with him, hence he crushed him with disease' (Isaiah 53:10).

"Is it possible that even if the victim did not accept the suffering with love, the same is so?

"Scripture states, 'To see if his soul would offer itself in restitution' (Isaiah 53:10).

"Just as the offering must be offered with the knowledge and consent [of the sacrificer], so sufferings must be accepted with knowledge and consent.

"If one accepted them in that way, what is his reward?

"'He will see his seed, prolong his days' (Isaiah 53:10).

"Not only so, but his learning will remain with him, as it is said, 'The purpose of the Lord will prosper in his hand' (Isaiah 53:10)."

Our task, when we suffer by reason of God's love, is to acknowledge and accept the suffering as a mark of God's favor. That difficult notion bears within itself a powerful source of healing, giving the suffering person power over his or her condition, turning pain into a source of intense meaning. Sages proceed now to help distinguish suffering brought on by God's love from other forms of suffering:

> R. Jacob bar Idi and R. Aha bar Hanina differed. One of them said, "What are sufferings brought on by God's love? They are any form of suffering which does not involve one's having to give up studying Torah.
>
> "For it is said, 'Happy is the man whom you chasten, O Lord, and yet teach out of your Torah' (Psalms 94:12)."
>
> The other said, "What are sufferings brought on by God's love? They are any form of suffering which does not involve having to give up praying.
>
> "For it is said, 'Blessed be God, who has not turned away my prayer nor his mercy from me' (Psalms 66:20)."
>
> Said to them R. Abba, son of R. Hiyya bar Abba, "This is what R. Hiyya bar Abba said R. Yohanan said, 'Both constitute forms of suffering brought on by God's love.
>
> "'For it is said, "For him whom the Lord loves he corrects"' (Proverbs 3:12)."

The purpose of this suffering is to take away sin, for, like a sacrifice for unwitting sin that is presented in the Temple in ancient times, suffering serves as an offering—when so intended:

> This furthermore accords with what R. Simeon b. Laqish said.
> For R. Simeon b. Laqish said, "A 'covenant' is stated in respect to salt, and a covenant is mentioned with respect to suffering.
>
> "With respect to a covenant with salt: 'Neither shall you allow the salt of the covenant of your God to be lacking' (Leviticus 2:13).
>
> "With respect to a covenant with suffering: 'These are the words of the covenant' (Deuteronomy 28:69) [followed by discourse on Israel's suffering].

"Just as the covenant noted with salt indicates that salt sweetens meat, so the covenant noted with suffering indicates that suffering wipes away all of a person's sins."

It has been taught on Tannaite authority:

Suffering, moreover, brings about divine favor; through suffering Israel is blessed with the three most important gifts God has to bestow: the Torah, the Land of Israel, and the life of the world to come or eternal life:

Simeon b. Yohai says, "Three good gifts did the Holy One, blessed be he, give to Israel, and all of them he gave only through suffering.

"These are they: Torah, the Land of Israel, and the world to come.

"How do we know that that is the case for Torah? As it is said, 'Happy is the man whom you chasten, O Lord, and teach out of your Torah' (Psalms 94:12).

"The Land of Israel? 'As a man chastens his son, so the Lord your God chastens you' (Deuteronomy 8:5), after which it is said, 'For the Lord your God brings you into a good land' (Deuteronomy 8:7).

"The world to come? 'For the commandment is a lamp and the teaching is light, and reproofs of sufferings are the way of life' (Proverbs 6:23)."

In this same context, suffering is deemed equivalent to acts of merit such as those of loving-kindness, study of the Torah, and the like: whoever buries his children is forgiven his sins, as much as one who devotes life to Torah-learning:

A Tannaite authority repeated the following statement before R. Yohanan: "Whoever devotes himself to study of the Torah or acts of loving kindness, [5B] or who buries his children, is forgiven all his sins."

Said to him R. Yohanan, "Now there is no issue with regard to study of the Torah or practice of deeds of loving kindness, for it is written, 'By mercy and truth iniquity is expiated' (Proverbs 16:6).

"'Mercy' refers to acts of loving kindness, for it is said, 'He who follows after righteousness and mercy finds life, prosperity, and honor' (Proverbs 21:21).

"'Truth' of course refers to Torah, for it is said, 'Buy the truth and do not sell it' (Proverbs 23:23).

"But how do we know that that is the case for one who buries his children?"

An elder repeated for him on Tannaite authority the following statement in the name of R. Simeon b. Yohai, "We draw an analogy to the sense of the word 'sin' used in several passages.

"Here it is written, 'By mercy and truth iniquity is expiated' (Proverbs 16:6), and elsewhere, 'And who repays the iniquity of the fathers into the bosom of their children' (Jeremiah 32:18)."

So much for the theory of matters. What about how the doctrine works itself out in the lives of the sages themselves? Here we come to a series of tales that make the same point. Holy saints of the Torah took a dim view of the idea of suffering as a precious gift: "neither them nor their reward." Here we see the human face of the Torah:

R. Hiyya bar Abba got sick. R. Yohanan came to him. He said to him, "Are these sufferings precious to you?"

He said to him, "I don't want them, I don't want their reward."

He said to him, "Give me your hand."

He gave him his hand, and [Yohanan] raised him up [out of his sickness].

Yohanan got sick. R. Hanina came to him. He said to him, "Are these sufferings precious to you?"

He said to him, "I don't want them. I don't want their reward."

He said to him, "Give me your hand."

He gave him his hand and [Hanina] raised him up [out of his sickness].

R. Eliezer got sick. R. Yohanan came to see him and found him lying in a dark room. [The dying man] uncovered his arm, and light fell [through the room]. [Yohanan] saw that R. Eliezer was weeping. He said to him, "Why are you crying? Is it because of the Torah that you did not learn sufficiently? We have learned: 'All the same are the ones who do much and do little, so long as each person will do it for the sake of heaven.'

"Is it because of insufficient income? Not everyone has the merit of seeing two tables [Torah and riches, as you have. You have been a master of Torah and also have enjoyed wealth].

"Is it because of children? Here is the bone of my tenth son [whom I buried, so it was no great loss not to have children, since you might have had to bury them]."

He said to him, "I am crying because of this beauty of mine which will be rotting in the ground."

He said to him, "For that it certainly is worth crying," and the two of them wept together.

In the course of time, he said to him, "Are these sufferings precious to you?"

He said to him, "I don't want them, I don't want their reward."

He said to him, "Give me your hand."

He gave him his hand, and [Yohanan] raised him up [out of his sickness].

Suffering involves not only illness but also loss of property or wealth:

Four hundred barrels of wine turned sour on R. Huna. R. Judah, brother of R. Sala the Pious, and rabbis came to see him (and some say it was R. Ada bar Ahba and rabbis). They said to him, "The master should take a good look at his deeds."

He said to them, "And am I suspect in your eyes?"

They said to him, "And is the Holy One, blessed be he, suspect of inflicting a penalty without justice?"

He said to them, "Has anybody heard anything bad about me? Let him say it."

They said to him, "This is what we have heard: the master does not give to his hired hand [the latter's share of] vine twigs [which are his right]."

He said to them, "Does he leave me any! He steals all of them to begin with."

They said to him, "This is in line with what people say: 'Go steal from a thief but taste theft too!' [Simon: If you steal from a thief, you also have a taste of it.]"

He said to them, "I pledge that I'll give them to him."

Some say that the vinegar turned back into wine, and some say that the price of vinegar went up so he sold it off at the price of wine.

Clearly, suffering expresses a certain rationality. But only within limits, and in the end, a more encompassing explanation would be required. That explanation derived from belief in the world to come.

Even sages treated with a measure of distance the doctrine of suffering as an expression of divine love. The full impact of the book of Job, with its conviction that Job's suffering—loss of his property, his children, and his health—in no way corresponded to Job's moral situation, certainly was felt by sages. Job's final reply surely meets with their approval, when he admits that "I spoke without understanding of things beyond me, which I did not know" (Job 42:3f). We cannot comprehend the fullness of creation, all the more so is our capacity to understand God's justice going to fail. But the one point at which sages will part company from Scripture is the brutal insistence of Qoheleth (Ecclesiastes), "For the same fate is in store for all: for the righteous and for the wicked, for the good and pure and for the impure . . ." (Qoheleth 9:2); "sometimes an upright man is required according to the conduct of the scoundrel, and sometimes the scoundrel is required according to the conduct of the upright" (Qoh. 8:14).

SUFFERING AND EVIL: THE LARGER QUESTION OF ETIOLOGY AND THEODICY

Suffering is not evil, and suffering does not originate in evil. Suffering represents a good, something to be valued. So the founders of holy Israel, Abraham, Isaac, and Jacob, are credited with asking God for sickness and old age:

> "When Isaac was old, and his eyes were dim, so that he could not see, he called Esau his older son, and said to him, 'My son,' and he answered, 'Here I am'" (Genesis 27:1):
>
> Said R. Judah bar Simon, "Abraham sought [the physical traits of] old age [so that from one's appearance, people would know that he was old]. He said before him, 'Lord of all ages, when a man and his son come in somewhere, no one knows whom to honor. If you crown a man with the traits of old age, people will know whom to honor.'
>
> "Said to him the Holy One, blessed be he, 'By your life, this is a good thing that you have asked for, and it will begin with you.'
>
> "From the beginning of the book of Genesis to this passage, there is no reference to old age. But when Abraham our father came along, the traits of old age were given to him, as it is said, 'And Abraham was old' (Genesis 24:1).
>
> "Isaac asked God for suffering. He said before him, 'Lord of the age, if someone dies without suffering, the measure of strict justice is stretched out against him. But if you bring suffering on him, the measure of strict justice will not be stretched out against

him. [Suffering will help counter the man's sins, and the measure of strict justice will be mitigated through suffering by the measure of mercy.]'

"Said to him the Holy One, blessed be he, 'By your life, this is a good thing that you have asked for, and it will begin with you.'

"From the beginning of the book of Genesis to this passage, there is no reference to suffering. But when Isaac came along, suffering was given to him: his eyes were dim.

"Jacob asked for sickness. He said before him, 'Lord of all ages, if a person dies without illness, he will not settle his affairs for his children. If he is sick for two or three days, he will settle his affairs with his children.'

"Said to him the Holy One, blessed be he, 'By your life, this is a good thing that you have asked for, and it will begin with you.'

"That is in line with this verse: 'And someone said to Joseph, "Behold, your father is sick"' (Gen. 48:1)."

Said R. Levi, "Abraham introduced the innovation of old age, Isaac introduced the innovation of suffering, Jacob introduced the innovation of sickness."

—Genesis Rabbah LXV:IX

Old age, suffering, sickness—these form the main beams of the human condition. They are not to be explained away, nor treated as trivial, but to be valued.

But what of martyrdom, unhappily a common experience for Israel, God's people, from the very beginning? And how to justify the fate of the martyrs? Enough has been said to indicate how Judaism will set forth its theodicy—its explanation of the righteousness of God in the face of the presence of evil in the world. But Judaism recognizes that in the end, suffering bears its own messages and is not to be turned aside or explained away, but accepted with dignity and love for God. That is the point of the story of Aqiba's martyrdom:

R. Aqiba was being tortured [lit.: being judged] by the evil
Tinneius Rufus. When [he was close to death,] the time to recite the Shema approached. He began to recite the Shema and
he smiled.

He [Tinneius] said to him, "Elder, either you are a sorcerer
[who does not feel pain] or you mock the torture [which I in-
flict upon you].

He [Aqiba] said to him, "Woe unto you. I am neither a sorcerer, nor a mocker. But [I now was thinking,] all my life when
I recited this verse, I was troubled and wondered when I would
be able to fulfill all three aspects [of this verse]: 'And you shall
love the Lord your God with all you heart, and with all your
soul, and with all your might' (Deuteronomy 6:5). I have
loved him with all my heart. And I have loved him with all my
wealth. But I did not know how I would [fulfill the verse and]
love him with all my soul.

"And now the time has come [for me to love him] with all
my soul, and the time has come to recite the Shema. It is now
clear to me [how I shall serve him with all my soul]. For this
reason I now am reciting and smiling." And just as he said this
his soul passed from him.

—Yerushalmi to tractate Berakhot 9:5/I:3

Through suffering we serve God with our very soul: a stern
message, but one commensurate to the question. As David
Kraemer remarks on this passage, "Aqiba did not rail against his
suffering but instead accepted it with joy."[5]

The problem of suffering and evil for contemporary Jews
transcends matters of theological theory. It is an everyday presence for us all, whether or not we practice Judaism. The century now drawing to a close marked the most difficult period in
the history of the Jewish people and of Judaism. What hap-
pened, as is well known, is that six million Jews were murdered
in death factories created by the German government for that

very purpose. The issue of the Holocaust draws us to a revision of the entire civilization of the West, which produced, as its most civilized country, the Germany that did these things. But it was not a Christian Germany, it was a National Socialist Germany, hostile to Christianity and to Judaism. How to construct a theodicy—a justification of God's ways—in the aftermath of the murder of six million men, women, and children is something no one knows. The task at hand demands a different gift: the grace to hope and not despair, to say, even in the twentieth century, Amen. Your will be done. And by going on with life, the Jewish people have said just that. We do not get to choose those with whom we shall share this earth or this age. So we accept what is meted out to us.

If in the end theodicy fails, that offers no excuse for atheism, and for every Jew who gave up the faith by reason of the Holocaust, ten Jews reaffirmed the faith and undertook to live all the more devotedly by its Torah. Jews who survived the concentration camps and gas chambers emerged, in vast proportion, with renewed commitment to God and the Torah. And that is because, in the end, attitude, not theodicy, decides matters. And the attitude of love for God, patient acceptance of what God metes out, above all, humble acknowledgment that, in the end, we may not ever fully understand the whys or wherefores—that attitude characterizes holy Israel, not only through all time, but today as well.

For a Jew it is a sin to despair. The Jews' assigned task within humanity has been to hope—despite and against it all to endure and abide in perfect faith and trust, to hope. Evil and suffering form the challenge; Israel, the model of humanity's response. After Auschwitz Israel, God's people, affirmed life. That is what it has meant to be Israel, "in our image, after our likeness." The critical Judaic component of the Christian civilization of the West spoke of God and God's will for humanity: the living God of Abraham, Isaac, and Jacob, not the God of the philosophers, not the construct of the theologians. The issue of the Torah is the issue of everyday life: what it means to live in God's image, after God's likeness. So said the Judaism of the dual Torah, so too said Christianity in its worship of God made flesh. So that message of humanity in God's image, of a people seeking to conform to God's will, found resonance in the Christian world as well: both components of the world, the Christian dough, the Judaic yeast, bore a single message about humanity.

We now live in an age in which people take for granted, as facts, the propositions of secularity and atheism. There is no problem of evil for atheism, only for monotheism. The century that draws to a close spoke of class and nation, not one humanity in the image of one God. Calling for heroes, it demanded sacrifice not for God but for the state. When asked what it meant to live with irreconcilable difference, the century of militant secularism and atheism responded with total war on civilians in their homes, made into foxholes. Asked to celebrate the image of humanity, the twentieth century created its improbable likeness of humanity: mountains of corpses, the dead of the Somme of World War I and of Auschwitz of World War II and all the other victims of the state that took the place of church and synagogue, even up to the one-third of the population of the Khmer killed by their own government, and the half of the world's Armenians by what, alas, was theirs, and the Jews and the Jews and the Jews.

The first century found its enduring memory in one man on a hill, on a cross; the twentieth, in six million making up a Golgotha—a mountain of skulls—of their own. Judaism has no answer to the problem of evil when that problem is framed in contemporary images. Nor should it. The Judaisms of the age struggled heroically to frame a Judaic system appropriate to the issues of the age—and failed. Who would want to have succeeded to frame a worldview congruent to such an age, a way of life to be lived in an age of death? No Judaic answer to the question of evil, no Judaic theodicy, could ever have found an enduring fit with an age such as the one that, at the turning of the century, draws to a close. Judaism struggled to speak to Israel, the Jewish people, of hope, of life in the valley of the darkest shadows. But Judaism had to fail, and that failure of relevance vindicates the Judaism of the dual Torah. For the Jews are a people that could find no place in such an age, no home in the twentieth century. And their religion, the Torah, also found no hearing. That, in the aspect of eternity, may prove the highest tribute God will pay to those among humanity whom God first chose through the Torah that he gave.

CHAPTER 5

Islam

WHY ARE EVIL, SUFFERING, AND PAIN A PROBLEM FOR ISLAM?

Within the complex of issues surrounding the question of evil and suffering, several problems arise for Islam. How, for instance, does Islam see the relationship of these distinct ideas, and how is suffering distinguished from ordinary pain? While pain is a universal phenomenon experienced by all humans and many other life forms, suffering requires a specific interpretation of pain. For instance, receiving an electric shock to my finger is painful, but if it occurred because I am careless while repairing a toaster, then it can hardly be called suffering (except, perhaps, to my ego). If, however, that shock is part of a program of torture by my enemy, then this same stimulus is clearly a case of suffering. For pain to be suffering, a particular set of circumstances is required, often including the loss of the ability to rectify the situation.

What makes suffering evil, however, is the malevolent intent of others, which is perceived to be outside the bounds of acceptable human behavior. If I shock myself, it is my own fault and I can avoid further pain by merely unplugging the toaster. If I am being tortured, however, someone else is both harming me and keeping me from being able to avoid further pain; for this reason, torture is recognized as unconscionable behavior, an evil to be eradicated. Muslims have endured their share of

suffering over the years, including war, poverty, and famine—
that is, situations in which Muslims have no control over their
destiny. In the Muslim worldview, however, famine is not necessarily evil, for there is no malevolent intent. As part of God's
creation, the world is an essentially good place in which both
suffering and pleasure occur. Such evil as there is in the world is
not derived either from God or from an evil "antigod"; rather,
Muslims see the roots of evil in the actions of others that step
outside the path that God has laid down.

The Qur'an itself helps to clarify the distinction between
suffering and evil in a curious story in which Moses meets up
with a mystical character known as "al-Khidr." Moses desires to
follow al-Khidr as he carries out God's will, but al-Khidr
prophesies that Moses would not be able to endure his rounds
patiently.

> [Moses and al-Khidr] departed; until, when they embarked upon
> the ship, he made a hole in it. [Moses] said, "What, hast thou
> made a hole in it so as to drown its passengers? Thou hast indeed
> done a grievous thing." Said he, "Did I not say that thou couldst
> never bear with me patiently?" [Moses] said, "Do not take me to
> task that I forgot, neither constrain me to do a thing too difficult."
>
> So they departed; until, when they met a lad, he slew him.
> [Moses] said, "What, hast thou slain a soul innocent, and that not
> to retaliate for a soul slain? Thou hast indeed done a horrible
> thing."
>
> —The Cave 18:70–74[1]

As the story continues, al-Khidr also rebuilds a ruined wall for
no apparent reason. Moses, of course, cannot refrain from
chastising him for this meaningless act, and al-Khidr tires of
Moses' impatience and leaves him. Before he departs, though,
he tells the secret of his actions:

As for the ship, it belonged to certain poor men, who toiled upon the sea; and I desired to damage it, for behind them there was a king who was seizing every ship by brutal force. As for the lad, his parents were believers; and we were afraid he would impose on them insolence and unbelief; so we desired that their Lord should give to them in exchange one better than he in purity, and nearer in tenderness. As for the wall, it belonged to two orphan lads in the city, and under it was a treasure belonging to them.

—The Cave 18:78–81[2]

This tale demonstrates the difficulty that Moses, God's chosen prophet, has in determining whether an act is really good or evil. Simply put, what may seem like suffering to some is actually God's way of alleviating greater suffering; therefore, the ultimate measure of evil has to do with perspective, because God does not will evil.

Since pain is not always suffering, and suffering is not always evil, it is easier to understand how some Muslims would choose to endure suffering for the sake of their religion. During the first decade of Islam, while Muhammad was preaching in Mecca, many of the first Muslims underwent substantial deprivations for their faith. Some were tortured and even killed. Ibn Hisham (d. 834) records the following story of Bilal, the Abyssinian slave who eventually became the first muezzin, or summoner to prayer:

Bilal the slave was one of those who bore the truth of Islam, being pure of heart. His master Umayyah b. Khalaf used to take him out during the hot afternoon and throw him on his back in the valley of Mecca; he would then call for a huge rock to be placed upon his chest. Then his master would say to him: "You will remain in this state until you either die or declare Muhammad to be an unbeliever and promise to serve the goddesses al-Lat and al-'Uzzah." Bilal, however, would cry out, "God is one, one!" in spite of this torture.

Abu Bakr passed by one day when they were doing this to Bilal, since Abu Bakr's house was near those of Umayyah's tribe. So Abu Bakr said to Umayyah b. Khalaf: "Do you not fear God for what you are doing to this poor soul? How long will you continue?" Umayyah replied: "You are the one who ruined him, so you deliver him from the torture you see here!" Abu Bakr said: "I'll do it; I have a black slave stronger than he and an adherent of your faith—I'll give him to you in exchange for Bilal." Umayyah responded: "I accept." So Abu Bakr exchanged the slaves, took Bilal and freed him.

—Ibn Hisham, *Sirah*, 1:339–40[3]

Bilal's willingness to endure pain for the sake of Islam is an example of how the individual suffering of one Muslim is put into the context of the general health of all Muslims. But Abu Bakr also plays an important role here in rescuing God's faithful servant. So while Muslims may choose to endure suffering for the sake of the religion, they should also act to relieve the suffering of others.

A second problem to be addressed is the origin of suffering and evil. According to Muslim belief, God is the source of all things, and the Qur'an waxes eloquent in urging the unbelievers to understand rain, crops, and cattle as gifts of a benevolent God. In a way, however, the Qur'an is setting up two seemingly contradictory propositions: (1) God is omnipotent and all-powerful, and nothing happens without his making it happen; (2) God is loving and caring, and wishes the best for his servants. These propositions work well when we are speaking of good things like rain and wealth, but are famine and poverty also from God, or do they exist apart from his will?

This is precisely the question that fueled a great theological debate for centuries. The earliest discernible position in this debate is that of theologians who held to a strict fatalism, seeing all actions foreordained by a blind sense of fate. Their position is expressed in this *hadith*, which is found in Ibn Hanbal's collection:

> The first thing God created was the Pen; then he said to it, "Write!" It asked, "What shall I write?" He said, "Write what will be and what is in being until the coming of the Hour!"

This hadith contrasts with the Qur'an, not only in limiting the efficacy of the believers' actions, but also in describing God's actions. Rather than the personally involved overseer of human affairs, God is more a bystander in this hadith. The work of determination, even that of changing the very nature of a person, is done by an impersonal object, as can be seen in a second hadith from al-Bukhari's collection: "Then the angel is sent to the womb and breathes the Spirit into the fetus. Four words are commanded: to write down its sustenance, its time of death, its acts, and 'damned' or 'blessed.'" This hadith recalls the Aristotelian process of "ensoulment," and it suggests that one's life is completely determined from before birth, with all one's actions written down in a heavenly book. Such a position, however, does not square with Qur'anic descriptions of judgment day, at which souls will be questioned for their deeds; if acts are "written down" when the person is still in the womb, then how could anyone be punished for committing them? In opposition to this opinion, a group called the Mu'tazilites strove to remove evil from God, understanding all evil to arise from human rebellion against God. In this scheme, God is pure justice and goodness, while the present world is a corruption of God's will. Not surprisingly, the resolution adopted by al-Ash'ari (d. 935) falls somewhere between these two positions. In a rather complicated passage, he states:

> God created the creatures free from unbelief and from belief. . . . God did not compel any of his creatures to be infidels or faithful.

And he did not create them either as faithful or infidels, but he created them as individuals, and faith and unbelief are the acts of human beings. All the acts of human beings . . . are truly their own acquisition, but God creates them.[4]

This passage will be explored in more detail below, but what is interesting for our discussion is to identify the problem with which al-Ash'ari is dealing. Evil acts, as well as good ones, must be created by God, since suggesting that anyone else creates them would be setting up a rival to God's creative power. Nevertheless, al-Ash'ari also holds that "faith and unbelief are the acts of human beings," meaning that individual Muslims are culpable for their actions. In a sense, al-Ash'ari solves the problem by asserting this paradox: God is the source of all acts, but evil acts only come from human beings. As will be seen below, this is a very productive problem, and the theologians will not have the last word.

A third problem arises when one looks at the multitude of ways that Muslims deal with pain itself. Of course, Muslims spend most of their lives avoiding pain—some of the world's greatest doctors are Muslims, and much of European medicine is directly based on the advances that medieval Muslim doctors, like the famous Avicenna, made over ancient Greek medicine. But like adherents of other religions, Muslims may seek out pain as a way of turning their focus away from what the Qur'an calls "the chance goods of this world," and turning toward God. The most obvious example of such pain is in the yearly fast at Ramadan. During an entire month, Muslims do not consume anything—food, drink, or cigarettes—during the daylight hours. The discipline of denying oneself sustenance during the day helps Muslims to focus on God as the real source of that sustenance. Nevertheless, this pain is to be kept within certain boundaries, and those who are sick, traveling, or pregnant are not required to fast.

Another example of how pain is actually sought out by Muslims is in the Shiʿite ritual of *taʿziyyah*. Shiʿites differ from Sunnites primarily in their attitude toward the family of the Prophet. While all Muslims venerate the Prophet's grandsons and other descendants, Shiʿites believe that the first twelve descendants (known as the Imams) had a specific calling to lead all Muslims—a calling that was ignored by Sunnites. The third Imam, the Prophet's grandson Husayn, died with some seventy followers in a skirmish with the ruling Umayyad Caliphs in 680 C.E. This battle is reenacted in Shiʿite countries in a type of passion play. Moreover, parades commemorate the event and some groups of men beat themselves with chains and knives, crying out for the untimely death of the Prophet's grandson and sharing in his pain. The "problem" of pain and suffering in these cases is that pain is viewed positively in these traditions, and suffering in this world is seen as a path to ease and comfort in the world to come.

In isolating these three problems—the relation of suffering to evil; the origin of suffering and evil; and Muslim responses to suffering—it should be obvious that the Islamic religion sets up an interpretive framework that helps Muslims make sense of all kinds of phenomena, and pain and suffering are no exception. As we delve further into this material, however, one should also keep in mind that *our* notions of suffering and evil are also determined by our cultural environment. The question is not how do Muslims deal with what we perceive as suffering, but rather how do Muslims make sense of their own responses to pain.

HOW IS SUFFERING REPRESENTED AND PERCEIVED AND EXPERIENCED?

The most vivid representations of suffering in the Qur'an are the torturous scenes of sinners languishing in hell. Especially in the Meccan suras, when Muhammad was preaching to a crowd of skeptical polytheists, vivid depictions of hell abound:

The Companions of the Left (O Companions of the Left!)
mid burning winds and boiling waters
and the shadow of a smoking blaze
neither cool, neither goodly;
and before that they lived in ease,
and persisted in the Great Sin, ever saying,
"What, when we are dead and become dust and bones, shall we
indeed be raised up?
What, and our fathers, the ancients?"
Say: "The ancients, and the later folk shall be gathered to the appointed time of a known day.
Then you erring ones, you that cried lies,
you shall eat of a tree called Zakkoum,
and you shall fill therewith your bellies
and drink on top of that boiling water
lapping it down like thirsty camels."

—The Terror, 56:40–55[5]

Here, even the words of the skeptical polytheists are preserved
by the Qur'an as they ask how God will bring back to life the
very bones that can be seen in the desert. The Qur'an calls these
challenges to its message "crying lies," and sees hell as a fitting
end for these people. Other descriptions pick up these same
themes.

Faces on that day humbled,
labouring, toilworn,
roasting at a scorching fire,
watered at a boiling fountain,
no food for them but cactus thorn
unfattening, unappeasing hunger.

—The Enveloper, 88:2–76

In these passages, the Qur'an is tailoring its description to the desert-dwelling Meccans, describing for them a hell of suffering that mimics and intensifies the pain of life in the Arabian desert. The burning heat of the desert sun is increased by fire, and the thirsty receive only boiling water or melted copper to drink.

These harsh tales of eternal damnation were a response to the lack of belief in hell among the Meccans. When the unbelievers say, "Shall we indeed be raised up?" they are doubting the very existence of an afterlife, claiming, "There is nothing but our present life; we die, and we live, and nothing but Time destroys us." To this skepticism, the Qur'an responds with vivid imagery of hellfire, saying that the Meccans "have no knowledge; they merely conjecture" (45:23). The Qur'an does not merely replace old Arab concepts of destiny with God, but sees God as a different kind of active principle in the world, as the author of life and death. In a sense, the Qur'an uses depictions of suffering to turn the Meccan world upside down, warning that ease in this world may actually lead to suffering in the next.

Evil in the Qur'an is less clearly defined than suffering. Like other monotheistic religions, Islam cannot blame evil on a powerful "antigod," since there is only one creative force in the universe, and the existence of a rival to God would compromise God's absolute power. Nevertheless, devils of a sort exist in Islam, both in the person of Iblis and in the form of spirits of fire called *jinn*. These jinn have a definite tendency toward evil and are to be avoided as much as possible. The Qur'an also refers to both Satan, who appears to be the same as Iblis, and satans, who appear to be the same as jinn.

The most important passage in the Qur'an regarding Iblis concerns the creation of the first human being, when Iblis refused to bow down to the new creature, even though God had commanded it:

> Surely We created man of a clay of mud moulded,
> and the jinn created We before of fire flaming.

And when thy Lord said to the angels, "See, I am creating a
mortal of a clay of mud moulded.

When I have shaped him, and breathed My spirit in him, fall
you down, bowing before him!"

Then the angels bowed themselves all together, save Iblis; he
refused to be among those bowing.

Said He, "What ails thee, Iblis, that thou art not among those
bowing?" Said he, "I would never bow myself before a mortal
whom Thou hast created of a clay of mud moulded."

Said He, "Then go thou forth hence; thou art accursed.

Upon thee shall rest the curse, till the Day of Doom."

Said he, "My Lord, respite me till the day they shall be raised."

Said He, "Thou art among the ones that are respited unto the
day of a known time."

Said he, "My Lord, for Thy perverting me I shall deck fair to
them in the earth,

and I shall pervert them, all together,

excepting those Thy servants among them that are devoted."

Said He, "This is for me a straight path: over My servants
thou shalt have no authority, except those that follow thee, being
perverse."

—Al-Hijr 15:26–41[7]

From this story, which is told many times throughout the
Qur'an, we learn several important facts about evil. First, evil
may be defined as a perversion of God's will—even God's just
punishment against Iblis is converted, in Iblis's eyes, to perversion. In a sense, this is the same message as that told in the story
of Moses and al-Khidr: in both cases, God's will is good and
just, but faulty human (or devilish) perception makes it seem
otherwise.

A second point in this story has to do with the way that evil
works in a person's life. In a combination of free will and fatalism, Iblis and God agree that those who choose to follow God's

straight path will be immune to Iblis's trickery, while those who choose to follow Iblis once will be under his power. Along these lines, it is interesting to note that Iblis himself was able to refuse God's command; he is not portrayed as an automaton who cannot move against God's will. Later Muslim theologians will explain that this freedom of choice was given to Iblis by God, but regardless, he is allowed to act against God.

Finally, though, Iblis is not a personification of evil, nor is he to blame for the pain and suffering of human existence. Iblis may trick human beings into doing evil, but evil results from human action. Even the prophet Muhammad fell prey to Iblis's role as "the slinking whisperer" when he whispered false verses into the Prophet's ear. These verses, in which the Prophet was tricked into praising three of the pre-Islamic goddesses, were corrected by a later revelation from God, and henceforth known as the Satanic Verses (from which Salman Rushdie borrowed the title to his famous book). The last sura of the Qur'an is an ancient prayer against the power of this trickster:

> In the Name of God, the Merciful, the Compassionate
> Say: "I take refuge with the Lord of men,
> the King of men,
> the God of men,
> from the evil of the slinking whisperer
> who whispers in the breasts of men
> of jinn and men."
>
> —Men 114:1–78

It may be surprising to read here that the "slinking whisperer" tricks both humankind and jinn into deeds of evil. The jinn, as it turns out, can also be believers or unbelievers, and one sura of the Qur'an (entitled: The Jinn) tells the story of a band of jinn who heard Muhammad preaching and became Muslims.

As a final note on Iblis, it should be mentioned that some

Muslims have characterized him as essentially good and not evil at all. Certain Muslim mystics of the ninth century saw in his refusal to bow to humankind a firm commitment to God's absolute unity. That is, Iblis refused to bow because no one deserved his worship other than God. This strange vindication of Iblis's actions can be seen as continuing a mystical tradition of looking for a deeper meaning behind mere appearances. But it also fits in with the mystical conception of the origin of evil in the *nafs*, or the lower soul of each human being. This nafs is the locus of base desires that must be vigilantly held in check. In fact, a war of sorts, called the *jihad al-nafs*, was postulated between the believer and these desires. The great theologian al-Ghazzali (d. 1111) wrote:

> The first meaning of nafs is the broad one: the human being's ability to become angry or lustful, according to that which will be explained. This usage of the word nafs is the most common among the sufis, because by the nafs, they mean the broadest characterization of evil human characteristics. They say: "there is no escaping the *jihad al-nafs* and its final destruction," and this is the explanation of the Prophet's statement (peace be upon him): "wage war against the enemy of your nafs, which resides within you."
>
> —*Iḥyā' 'ulūm al-dīn* 3:59

This doctrine found its way into mainstream Islam, to the point that Muslims understand war against the unbeliever to be the "lesser jihad," with the "greater jihad" being the battle against one's own self.

The final source of evil in Islam is, in some ways, both the most common and the easiest to overcome. Evil, and hence often pain and suffering, usually stems from the actions of others. As the Qur'an emphasizes in the story of Moses and al-Khidr, the proper response of the Muslim to suffering is patient endurance. Since Muslim histories are replete with examples of rulers who exploited the people and turned their suffering into material gain, patience appears to have been good advice. Yet the power of these rulers did not go unchallenged, and certain members of the community, such as the judges of the Islamic courts (*qadis*), were seen as the people's champions against this evil.

Muslim historical texts preserve numerous accounts of such qadis who were persecuted for their positions against corruption. One qadi, Sahnun (d. 856), became an example for later generations. At the meeting to elect a new qadi, Sahnun nominated someone else, refusing the nomination himself. But the ruler needed Sahnun to be the judge, since the people would trust no one else. When pressed by the local ruler, Sahnun delayed at least a year, forcing the ruler to accept a number of conditions, one of which was that he was to have leave to prosecute injustice, even into the ruling family itself. When these conditions were finally met and sworn upon, Sahnun reluctantly accepted the position:

> Muhammad b. Sahnun said: Sahnun was appointed to the judgeship after being pursued for a year, and he made it very difficult for the ruler, Muhammad b. al-Aghlab, who swore the most powerful oath to appoint him. So he was appointed on Monday, the third of Ramadan in the Muslim year of 234. Sahnun arose in those days, examining cases, and searching for assistants. Then the people came and sat before him on the Sunday after he was appointed in the central mosque, after he prostrated and prayed a great deal. Sahnun said: "It was not my idea to accept this position until I received from the ruler two assurances: the first being that he would give me all I asked and free my hands to investigate all I desired, even if I were to say to him: 'I will begin to inquire into the people of your house, your relatives and your assistants; some of them have been oppressors of the people and of their money for a long time, and they will remain so if the one who appeals to me is not encouraged to speak against them.' And the ruler responded

to me: 'Begin with them, and let justice rain down on the hair of my head.' I said: 'By God?' He answered: 'By God, three times.' So his determination was made clear to me in this, that no one should fear for themselves in front of the court. I thought about the matter and did not find anyone else who deserved this position, nor did I find in myself the ability to refuse him."

—Qadi 'Iyad, *Tartib* 1:596[10]

Sahnun's speech identifies the ruler and his family as the source of the people's suffering, but he also recognizes himself as the only person who can stand up to the ruler. Protection of the Muslim people against this evil has its cost, however, and Sahnun's arrogance disappears when he rides through the streets of Kairouan after accepting his post.

Sulayman b. Salim said: when the appointment of Sahnun was completed, the people went out to meet him, and I saw him riding on a riding animal, without cloak or cap. His face was grim, and no one was running to congratulate him. He went on like this until he came to his daughter Khadijah, who was among the best of women, and he said to her: "Today your father has been slaughtered without a knife."

—Qadi 'Iyad, *Tartib* 1:596–97[11]

As a qadi, Sahnun is well aware of the dangers facing him, yet he neither fears earthly power, nor does he allow earthly authority to trump religious authority. For the sake of the people, he admonishes the ruler and corrects him when necessary, even though these actions may lead to his own death. In fact, Sahnun's willingness to sacrifice himself for the good of the people is akin to the soldier fighting the jihad, since both give up their earthly life for the good of Islam.

Sahnun's jihad against an evil despot is akin to the sufis' jihad against their base desires. These two sources of evil—the evil intentions of others and the base desires of one's own soul—can be actively fought, although the third source, Iblis and his cohorts, requires someone with access to the unseen world. It is a Muslim's lot, then, to combat the evil that is a part of natural existence in this world in order to avoid the eternal suffering in the world to come, which will be imposed on those who turn away from God's path. None of this is to suggest that suffering is good, or even neutral, in the Islamic understanding; rather it is a part of the ordained existence of humankind, which is to be endured until God rewards the believer with eternal life in paradise.

WHY DOES SUFFERING MATTER, AND HOW DO WE DEAL WITH, OR OVERCOME, SUFFERING?

While God's will, and ultimately good and evil, may be hard for the individual Muslim to discern, Muslims are still expected to follow "the command to do good and the prohibition of doing evil." Moreover, the word for "good" in this formula (found in several places in the Qur'an) is *al-ma'ruf,* "the well-known," while "evil" is *al-munkar,* "the unknown." Continuing on this theme, the Qur'an calls itself *mubin,* "the clear word," and Islamic law itself is a straight, broad path, the *shari'ah.* This terminology suggests that good actions should be obvious to the Muslim, and that actions that are publicly accepted by the community of Muslims are, by definition, good. So, whatever question there may be about evil and suffering, good action should be clear, and the Muslim response to evil and suffering is to stay on God's path of right action.

Within this overall conceptual framework, there are many things that Muslims can do to ward off evil. These daily actions can be placed in two categories: those that increase one's piety and concentration on God, and those that actively deter evil. Fazlur Rahman (d. 1988), professor of Islamic thought at the University of Chicago for many years, describes the Muslim response to the temptations of Satan in terms of increasing one's *taqwa,* that is, one's God-given ability to recognize evil for what it is:

> It is all-important for man to recognize the footsteps of Satan for what they are, otherwise, it is extremely difficult, indeed impossible, for man to save himself from perdition. Thus, the real problem lies within man himself, for he is a blend of good and evil, ignorance and knowledge, power and impotence. The key to man's defense is *taqwa,* which literally means defense but which is a kind of inner light, a spiritual spark which man must light within himself to distinguish between right and wrong, seeming and real, immediate and lasting, etc. Once a human does this—and *taqwa* is, of course, capable of gradations—he should be able to see Satan's footsteps for what they are and not be beguiled by them.[12]

In this passage, Rahman rejects the argument that the human creature is powerless to resist the temptations of Satan; in fact, he regards Satan as essentially weak, able to prey only on those Muslims whose taqwa is also weak. Strengthening this "inner light" through prayer and right action provides an ability to recognize evil action and remove oneself from it.

Rahman also reiterates the fundamental point that evil does not originate with the devil, but with the tendencies of the human being to do evil. This is an important point, particularly in light of the way other religions perceive evil and suffering. While Christians, Hindus, and Buddhists may see the world as evil and a place of suffering, Muslims see the world as good, or at least neutral, with evil and suffering originating with humankind. As mentioned above, Muslim mystics (sufis) also perceive evil to originate not with Iblis, but within the lower soul (the nafs), which represents one's base desires. The sufi method for dealing with evil is also a defensive measure, similar to that of Rahman; both seek to develop the inner ability to perceive

God's will within the world and recognize evil for what it is. Therefore, the sufi maxim *shari'ah, tariqah, haqiqah* ("divine law, mystical path, divine reality") can be understood as another path for developing taqwa, beginning with the "well-known" actions enjoined by the shari'ah, then joining a sufi order and engaging in ritual prayer and other activities, with, finally, the hope of understanding divine reality.

Interestingly, some sufis maintained that this experience of divine reality could be sustained only for very short periods of time in this world, and after this ecstatic experience of unity with God, the practitioner is doomed to return. The sufis term this oscillation *fana'* ("annihilation" of the nafs, and union with God) and *baqa'* (persistence" in this experience of unity even after returning to this world). In this schema, suffering and evil serve as markers, which define existence in this world as opposed to the infinite good experienced in union with God. But the sufi adept who achieves the persistent unity of baqa' sees the suffering of this world to be nothing more than part of the myriad ways in which God manifests himself in creation.

The ability of sufi masters to perceive the real nature of evil in the world puts them in an excellent position to help other Muslims take active steps to ward off evil. In some countries, Muslims may seek amulets from a sufi sheikh to keep sickness at bay. These amulets are made from a variety of objects, including gold or silver pendants, on which are inscribed Qur'an verses or magical formulas; also popular is a pendant or earrings made into the shape of an open hand, known as the hand of Fatimah, the daughter of the Prophet. Amulets are thought to be particularly effective in warding off the influences of the jinn (the word for "insane" in Arabic is *majnun*; literally, "jinned") and the evil eye. Children and pregnant women are thought to be particularly prone to harm from the evil eye, which is connected with the envy of others. In some Muslim countries, old women may be blamed for a miscarriage or the death of a child, since they may be perceived as envious of another's ability to still bear children. Once again, the roots of these forms of evil and suffering are located in human action, and in turn, human action may be effective in keeping such evil away.

For Muslims, then, the struggle against evil and suffering does not take on any universal meaning, since God created the whole world *muslim,* or submissive to him. Rather, evil and suffering are fought on the everyday plane of this world. As for the evil intentions of others or the trickery of the jinn, amulets and the intervention of learned sheikhs form the best intervention. The more important struggle is the one within every Muslim, as he or she works to strengthen his or her own inner light through study and practice of the law. By keeping to the "well-known" actions of the shari'ah, each Muslim seeks to minimize the suffering that marks off this world from the world to come. It is interesting to note, however, that the five "pillars" of Islam—prayer, fasting, pilgrimage, confession of faith, and almsgiving—all have communal aspects, and some cannot be performed without the aid of other Muslims. This is a signal that one must not overemphasize the importance of individual action, since in the final reckoning, it is the community of Muslims that is the strongest proof against evil.

SUFFERING AND EVIL: THE LARGER QUESTION OF ETIOLOGY AND THEODICY

As mentioned above, the cause of evil and suffering in everyday life rests with a fundamental feature of the human being, who has tendencies to do good as well as evil. Iblis and the jinn have a similar tendency to do evil and to trick human beings into following them down the wrong path. But it is ultimately God who is the source of everything—so is God also the source of evil? This question proved very troubling for Muslim theologians, particularly of the ninth and tenth centuries, as some sought to remove God from evil while others claimed that doing so would compromise God's absolute oneness.

One solution to this problem is connected to the sufi ideas of fana' and baqa'. Union with God is understood as a process of traveling through myriad veils, leaving the diversity and suffering of this world behind and nearing the unity and perfection of God. Like Neoplatonic philosophers, Muslim mystics saw the universe as a series of domes over the earth, each a more perfect reflection of God. This scheme helps explain suffering and evil, since this world is the lowest sphere, the least perfect reflection of God's goodness. Parts of the Qur'an can be used to support this cosmology:

> And as for the unbelievers, . . . they are as shadows upon a sea obscure, covered by a billow, above which is a billow, above which are clouds, shadows piled one upon another.
>
> When he puts forth his hand, wellnigh he cannot see it. And to whomsoever God assigns no light, no light has he.
>
> —Light, 24:40–41[13]

This verse suggests that unbelievers do evil because they are separated from God, who himself is good. Yet while this view of the world explains much, it is still God who created the world in this way, who chooses those to whom light is to be assigned. Clearly the problem of God's association with evil could not be solved by merely describing the world, and Muslim theologians took up the task of explaining God's action within that world.

One of the oldest aspects of this debate is preserved in the following story from the *maqalat* of al-Ash'ari. Basically, Shu'ayb owes Maymun money, but is waiting to pay up until God wills it. When Maymun demands the money, Shu'ayb says, "If God had willed it, I could not have done otherwise." But Maymun says, "God has no will in respect of human acts;

human acts are not created by God." This debate opposes the old pre-Islamic fatalism against the new Islamic idea of placing responsibility for actions upon the individual. It seems that the fatalist view prevented the believer from any need to act on his or her own. But the response, a complete divorcing of God from the acts of human beings, will be seen as an unacceptable limitation on God's power.

Many other groups came up with responses to this problem in the first Islamic century. Among them were those who followed Shu'ayb's type of predestination, but asserted that God hated acts of disobedience. While this may not seem like much of a response, it will be deemed important enough to be included in the creeds of later scholars. Others took the notion of God's majesty to the extreme and suggested God's power was so great that human acts were merely a metaphor. With the arrival of this theory, we now have the full range of the debate as conceived by the Muslim theologians. On the one extreme, there is the notion that God has no part in human action; on the other, God's is the only action.

Not surprisingly, the debate about the relationship of God to evil involved all the major figures of the day, including the great legal scholar Ahmad b. Hanbal (d. 855). A creed attributed to Ahmad b. Hanbal still preserves a basic deterministic outlook, since it affirms the hadith mentioned above of God ordering the pen to write down all the acts of humanity. But it also appears to categorize the moral nature of human acts in such a way as to remove God from evil. According to this creed, sinful works are

Not in accordance with Allah's commandment, yet in accordance with His will; not in accordance with His desire, yet in accordance with His decision; not in accordance with His good pleasure, yet in accordance with His creation; not in accordance with His guidance; in accordance with His abandoning and His knowledge; yet not in accordance with His intimate awareness or with His writing on the preserved tablet.[14]

A clear attempt is made here to deal with Qur'anic language as it describes God's action. By differentiating between God's commandment and God's will, absolute power is maintained, as God's will is all-pervasive. Also preserved, however, is the essentially good nature of God, who cannot be seen as commanding an evil action. Additionally, the last statement suggests an attempt to understand the nature of the "preserved tablet" as merely a description of events to come, not a determination of individual sinful works.

Theologians of later generations became more and more creative as they tried to describe the particular way that evil could occur without God's causing it. Some argued that God created a moment of freedom to allow the human agent to choose which act to do, the good one or the evil one. Once that decision was made, God caused that act to take place. Another theologian, the famous al-Ash'ari (d. 935), distinguished between two types of events that "take place" in the human being. The first occurs in us through God's act alone, referring to nonvoluntary actions such as breathing and blinking. The second type refers to conscious acts, which we do intentionally "through an ability to act created in us at the moment the act occurs." This formulation gives the human just enough power to have culpability for the act, but no more. Al-Ash'ari was also the author of the creed quoted earlier in this chapter:

God created the creatures free from unbelief and from belief. . . . God did not compel any of his creatures to be infidels or faithful. And he did not create them either as faithful or infidels, but he created them as individuals, and faith and unbelief are the acts of human beings.[15]

Taken with the above doctrines, it is clear that God does work in terms of justice and grace, but that the meaning of these terms should not be deduced from human experience but from God's action in the world.

In reflecting on this debate, which raged for some three centuries, it is interesting to note the gradual progression to a more systematized and rational solution. The issues did not change radically over time, but the emphasis on creating a system did. Throughout, it was denied that God could act in a capricious or truly evil way. But by building a rational framework for understanding God's actions, the theologians seemed to be suggesting that God must conform to logic.

Finally, the problem of evil and suffering has two aspects for Muslims: what the existence of these things means for humankind, and what it means for God. In both cases, a paradox is revealed. On the one hand, Muslims see the world as basically good, the perfect creation of God, yet at the same time, the ills of poverty, famine, and plague in this world are as real in Muslim countries as they are elsewhere. Like Moses, though, the Muslim is to accept this apparent suffering as part of God's unlimited knowledge and justice, yet this should not lead to resignation, since like Abu Bakr and Sahnun they should act to alleviate suffering wherever possible. A similar paradox is found in the fact that God is unquestionably good and just, yet God is all-powerful and nothing happens without his leave. While some Muslim theologians attempted to solve this paradox with logic, the point of the paradox may be to demonstrate the ultimate inadequacy of the human mind to explain God's action. Indeed, other theologians merely asserted that both propositions were true *bila kayf,* without knowing how. Therefore contemplation of the problems of evil and suffering in Islam can lead Muslims to conclude that they, as humans, are inadequate to the task of conceiving God's purpose, and conversely, that God's mind is unfathomable.

APPENDIX: LITERARY SOURCES OF THE WORLD RELIGIONS

JUDAISM

Judaism, the religion, identifies as its authoritative source "the Torah," or "the teaching," defined as God's revelation to Moses at Sinai. Writings deemed canonical enter the category of Torah, though into that same category also fall all authentic teachings of every age. The revelation myth of Judaism maintains that at Sinai God revealed the Torah in two media, written and oral. That is to say, while part of the revelation took written form, another part was formulated orally and transmitted through memorization. The tradition of Sinai may then come to concrete expression through any great sage's teaching. But the account of the position of Judaism set forth in these pages derives from the dual Torah, written and oral, as set forth in the Hebrew Scriptures and as interpreted by "our sages of blessed memory," the rabbis of the first seven centuries of the common era.

The Written Part of the Torah
We know the written part of the Torah as the Hebrew Scriptures of ancient Israel, or the "Old Testament." This is made up of the Pentateuch, or Five Books of Moses (Genesis, Exodus, Leviticus, Numbers, and Deuteronomy); the Former Prophets (Joshua, Judges, Samuel, and Kings); the Latter Prophets (Isaiah, Jeremiah, and Ezekiel); the Twelve Minor Prophets; and the Writings (Psalms, Proverbs, Job, Song of Songs (aka the Song of Solomon), Ruth, Lamentations, Ecclesiastes, Esther, Daniel, Ezra, Nehemiah, and Chronicles). All translations from the written Torah come from the Revised Standard Version of the Bible.

The Oral Part of the Torah:
The Mishnah, Tosefta, and Two Talmuds
Judaism identifies a philosophical law code called the Mishnah
(c. 200 C.E.) as the first and most important of the finally tran-
scribed components of the oral Torah. The Mishnah is a set of
rules in six parts, made up of laws dealing with the hierarchical
classification of holy Israel in these categories: (1) agricultural
life; (2) the holy calendar, Sabbaths, and festivals; (3) women
and family; (4) civil law and the administration of justice and
the state; (5) the Temple and its offerings; (6) purity laws. A
tractate, or compilation of teachings, called Abot, "the Fathers," attached to the Mishnah commences, "Moses received
Torah at Sinai and handed it on to Joshua, Joshua to elders, and
elders to prophets. And prophets handed it on to the men of
the great assembly," and onward down to the very authorities
of the Mishnah itself. That is how the document is placed
within the oral tradition of Sinai. In addition to the Mishnah,
three other writings carry forward the legal tradition of Sinai:
the Tosefta (c. 300 C.E.), a set of further legal traditions in the
model of those in the Mishnah; the Talmud of the Land of Israel (c. 400 C.E.), a systematic amplification of thirty-nine of
the Mishnah's sixty-two topical tractates; and the Talmud of
Babylonia (c. 600 C.E.), a commentary to thirty-seven of the
same. The two Talmuds treat in common the second, third,
and fourth divisions of the Mishnah. The former takes up the
first; the latter, the fifth; and neither addresses the sixth. In addition, tractate Abot receives its Talmud in a compilation, *The
Fathers according to Rabbi Nathan,* of indeterminate date.

The Oral Part of the Torah: Midrash-Compilations
The work of commenting on the Mishnah and its legal traditions found its counterpart, among the same sages or rabbis, in
the labor of commenting on books of the written Torah. This

work produced Midrash, or exegesis, meaning the interpretation of Scripture in light of contemporary events by appeal to a
particular paradigm, or pattern, that showed how Scripture imposed meaning on contemporary occasions. Those biblical
books selected for intensive amplification are the ones read in
the synagogue: Genesis, in Genesis Rabbah (c. 400 C.E.); Exodus, in Mekhilta Attributed to Rabbi Ishmael (of indeterminate
date but possibly in c. 350 C.E.); Leviticus, in Sifra (c. 350 C.E.),
and also in Leviticus Rabbah (c. 450 C.E.); Numbers, in Sifré to
Numbers; and Deuteronomy, in Sifré to Deuteronomy (both c.
350 C.E.). In addition, Midrash-Compilations serve four of the
scrolls read in synagogue worship: Lamentations, read on the
9th of Ab to commemorate the destruction of the Temple; Esther, read on Purim; Song of Songs, read on Passover; and
Ruth, read on Pentecost. The Mishnah, Tosefta, Talmuds, and
Midrash-Compilations together form the authoritative canon
of Judaism in its formative age, the first seven centuries of the
common era. All translations of portions of the oral Torah
come from those made by the author.

CHRISTIANITY

The Christian faith understands itself to be grounded in the
Holy Spirit, God's self-communication. Access to the Holy
Spirit is possible because in Jesus Christ God became human.
The incarnation (God becoming flesh, *caro* in Latin) is what
provides the possibility of the Divine Spirit becoming acces-
sible to the human spirit.

Speaking from the perspective of Christian faith, then, there
is a single source of theology: the Holy Spirit, which comes
from the Father and Son. But the inspiration of the Holy Spirit
has been discovered and articulated by means of distinct kinds
of literature in the history of the church. By becoming aware of
the diversity of those sources, we can appreciate both the variety and the coherence of Christianity.

The Scriptures of Israel have always been valued within the church, both in Hebrew and in the Greek translation used in the Mediterranean world. (The Greek rendering is called the Septuagint, after the seventy translators who were said to have produced it.) Those were the only scriptures of the church in its primitive phase, when the New Testament was being composed. In their meetings of prayer and worship, followers of Jesus saw the Scriptures of Israel "fulfilled" by their faith: their conviction was that the same Spirit of God that was active in the prophets was, through Christ, available to them.

The New Testament was produced in primitive communities of Christians to prepare people for baptism, to order worship, to resolve disputes, to encourage faith, and for like purposes. As a whole, it is a collective document of primitive Christianity. Its purpose is to call out and order true Israel in response to the triumphant news of Jesus' preaching, activity, death, and resurrection. The New Testament provides the means of accessing the Spirit spoken of in the Scriptures of Israel. Once the New Testament was formed, it was natural to refer to the Scriptures of Israel as the "Old Testament."

The Old Testament is classic for Christians because it represents the ways in which God's Spirit might be known. At the same time, the New Testament is normative: it sets out how we actually appropriate the Spirit of God, which is also the spirit of Christ. That is why the Bible as a whole is accorded a place of absolute privilege in the Christian tradition: it is the literary source from which we know both how the Spirit of God has been known and how we can appropriate it.

"Early Christianity" (between the second and the fourth centuries of the common era) designates the period during which the church founded its theology on the basis of the scriptures of the Old and New Testaments. Although Christians were under extreme—sometimes violent—pressure from the Roman Empire, Early Christianity was a time of unique creativity. From thinkers as different from one another as Bishop Irenaeus in France and Origen, the speculative teacher active first in Egypt and then in Palestine, a common Christian philosophy began to emerge. Early Christianity might also be called a "catholic" phase, in the sense that it was a quest for a "general" or "universal" account of the faith, but that designation may lead to confusion with Roman Catholicism at a later stage, and is avoided here.

After the Roman Empire itself embraced Christianity in the fourth century, the church was in a position to articulate formally its understanding of the faith by means of common standards. During this period of Orthodox Christianity, correct norms of worship, baptism, creeds, biblical texts, and doctrines were established. From Augustine in the West to Gregory of Nyssa in the East, Christianity for the first and only time in its history approached being truly ecumenical.

The collapse of Rome under the barbarian invasions in the West broke the unity of the church. Although the East remained wedded to the forms of Orthodoxy (and accepts them to this day), the West developed its own structure of governance and its own theology, especially after Charlemagne was crowned as Emperor of the Romans by Pope Leo III on Christmas day in 800 C.E. European Christianity flourished during the Middle Ages, and Scholastic theology was a result of that success.

The Scholastics were organized on the basis of educational centers, Thomas Aquinas at the University of Paris during the thirteenth century being the best example. During the periods of Early Christianity and Orthodoxy, theologies as well as forms of discipline and worship were developed for the first time. Scholastic theology was in the position of systematizing these developments for the usage of the West. At the same time, Scholastic theologians also rose to the challenge of explaining Christian faith in the terms of the new philosophical movements they came into contact with.

The Reformation, between the sixteenth and the eighteenth centuries, challenged the very idea of a single system of Christianity. Martin Luther imagined that each region might settle on its own form of religion. In England the settlement was on a national basis, while in John Calvin's Geneva the elders of the city made that determination. But in all its variety, the Reformation insisted that the Bible and worship should be put into the language of the people, and that their governance should be consistent with their faith.

From the eighteenth century until the present, Christianity in its modern form has been wrestling with the consequences of the rise of rationalism and science. The results have been diverse and surprising. They include Protestant Fundamentalism—a claim that the Bible articulates certain "fundamentals," which govern human existence—and the Roman Catholic idea of papal infallibility, the claim that the pope may speak the truth of the church without error. In both cases, the attempt is made to establish an axiom of reason that reason itself may not challenge. But modern Christianity also includes a vigorous acceptance of the primacy of individual judgment in the life of communities: examples include the Confessing Church in Germany, which opposed the Third Reich, and the current movement of liberation theology in Central and South America.

Today Christians may use many combinations of the sort of sources named here to articulate their beliefs, and the resulting pattern is likely to be as distinctive as what has been produced in the past.

ISLAM

The Qur'an

The single source that constitutes the basis of all inquiry into the religion of Islam is the Qur'an. Revealed to the prophet Muhammad from 610 to 632 C.E., it is understood as God's own speech. That is to say, Muslims believe that the Qur'an is not merely inspired by God, it is exactly what God meant to say to the early Muslim community and to the world in general. Furthermore, God spoke to Muhammad (usually through the angel Gabriel) in Arabic, and to this day Muslims resist translation of the Qur'an into any other language. The Qur'an is about as long as the Christian New Testament. It is divided into 114 chapters (called *suras*), which range in size from a few verses to a few hundred. All but one of these suras begin with an invocation, "In the name of God, the Merciful, the Compassionate," and with these words pious Muslims begin all endeavors of importance. There are many translations of the Qur'an into English; that of A. J. Arberry[1] is widely recognized as the best and will be used in this series, despite the unfortunate gender bias in Arberry's language.

The Qur'an describes itself as a continuation and perfection of a tradition of revelation that began with the Torah, revealed to the Jews, and the Gospels, revealed to the Christians. In fact, the Qur'an directly addresses Jews and Christians, urging them to put aside their differences and join Muslims in the worship of the one, true God: "Say: People of the Book! Come now to a word common between us and you, that we serve none but God" (The House of Imran 3:56). Jesus and Moses are explicitly recognized as prophets, and the rules and pious regulations in the Qur'an fit in well with similar rules found in Judaism and Christianity. Of course, a special role is given to Muhammad, the seal of the prophets and the leader of the early Muslim community.

Sunna: The Prophet as Text

The prophet Muhammad serves as the second "text" for Muslims. Unlike the Qur'an, which is the single source for God's divine word in Islam, the words and deeds of the Prophet are found in many different sources. When it comes to the Prophet, precise words are not as important as his general "way of doing things"; in Arabic, this is called the Prophet's *sunna*. The prophet Muhammad ibn 'Abd Allah was born almost six centuries after Jesus' birth, around 570 C.E., and for the first forty years of his life he organized trading caravans. Around the year 610, he began meditating in a cave near his hometown of Mecca. During these meditations he was overwhelmed by a vision of the angel Gabriel commanding him, "Recite!" This event changed his life forever and he began, slowly, to preach to his relatives and neighbors. After years of effort, Muhammad and a small group of followers moved to the town of Medina. This *hijrah,* the emigration of Muslims from Mecca to Medina in 622 C.E., marks the beginning of the Muslim calendar and was a turning point for the early community. In Medina, hundreds flocked to the new religion, and when the Prophet died in 632, he left behind thousands of believers. The survival of this early group is testified to by the almost one billion Muslims in the world today. Now, as then, Muslims see the Prophet as an example of the ideal believer. Muslims often name their boys after the Prophet, wear clothes like his, and try to live according to his precepts.

Hadith: Examples of the Prophet's Sunna

Muhammad's words and deeds were preserved and passed on from generation to generation in a form of oral transmission known as hadith. The Arabic word *hadith* means "story," and a typical hadith begins with a list of those from whom the story was received, going back in time to the Prophet. Following this list is the story itself, often an account of the Prophet's actions in a particular situation or the Prophet's advice on a certain problem. The list of transmitters is an integral part of the hadith; for example: "al-Qasim—'A'ishah—The Prophet said . . ." Here, al-Qasim (an early legal scholar) transmitted this hadith from 'A'ishah (one of the Prophet's wives), who heard it directly from the Prophet. These stories were quite popular among early generations of Muslims, but no one attempted to collect and organize them until over a hundred years after the Prophet's death. Two important early collections of hadith are those by al-Bukhari (d. 870) and Muslim ibn al-Hajjaj (d. 875). Hadith are also found in works of history and in commentaries on the Qur'an. It is worth emphasizing that Muslims do not believe that Muhammad was divine. A careful distinction was maintained between divine words, which originated with God and therefore were put into the Qur'an, and Muhammad's general advice to his community. Both sets of words were spoken by the Prophet, but the first were written down and carefully preserved, while the second were handed down through the more informal vehicle of hadith.

Tafsir: Commentary on the Texts

Today, as in previous ages, Muslims often turn directly to the Qur'an and hadith for guidance and inspiration, but just as often they turn to commentaries and interpretations of these primary sources. These commentaries concern themselves with questions of grammar, context, and the legal and mystical implications of the text. They expand the original source, often collecting interpretations of many previous generations together. The results can be massive. The Qur'an, for instance, is only one volume, but a typical commentary can be twenty volumes or more. The importance of commentary in the Islamic tradition demonstrates that the Qur'an and sunna of the Prophet are not the only sources of guidance in Islam. Rather, Muslims have depended on learned men and women to interpret the divine sources and add their own teachings to this tradition. Therefore, these commentaries are valuable sources for understanding the religious beliefs of Muslims throughout the ages. Together with the Qur'an and hadith, they provide a continuous expression of Islamic religious writing from scholars, mystics, and theologians from over fourteen centuries.

BUDDHISM

Upon examining the major bodies of sacred literature in Buddhism, it must first be noted that Buddhism does not define "canon" in the same sense that the Judaic, Christian, and Islamic religions do. First of all, scriptures comprising a Buddhist canon are not deemed authoritative on the basis of being regarded as an exclusive revelation granted to humans by a supreme divine being. In principle, the ultimate significance of a given scriptural text for Buddhists lies less in the source from whom it comes, or in the literal meanings of its words, than in its ability to generate an awakening to the true nature of reality. Texts are principally valued according to their ability to enable one to engage in practices leading to an enlightened state of salvific insight, which liberates one from suffering, although they can also be utilized to serve other vitally important if less ultimate purposes, such as the cultivation of compassionate ethics, explication of philosophical issues, and protection from obstacles to personal well-being. Buddhism is also distinctive in that it has never established any one body that has functioned in an equivalent manner to the Rabbinate, Episcopate, or Caliphate, charged with the determination of a single, fixed, closed list of authoritative works for the entire tradition. On a local level, Buddhist canons, based on the hermeneutical standard of privileging the realization of enlightenment over source and word, have tended to remain open (to varying degrees) to the inclusion of new scriptures over the course of history.

It should not be concluded that the factors discussed above have ever substantially limited the amount of sacred literature produced in Buddhism, or have relegated scripture to a status less than primary in the religion's history. On the contrary, the various major Buddhist collections of scripture are extraordinarily voluminous in size[2] and have continuously occupied a most highly revered place in the tradition as primary sources of teaching. Appeals to a scripture's provenance have indeed played a momentous role in Buddhist history, with a primary determinate of a text's canonicity being recognition of it as containing *buddha-vacana,* the "spoken word" of a Buddha, or enlightened being—usually Siddhartha Gautama, or Shakyamuni Buddha (563–483 B.C.E.)—the Indian founder of the religion. To reiterate, one can be sure that the authority assigned to buddha-vacana is derived in part from its source, but what is of utmost import is its liberating power as an indicator of enlightened wisdom.

Insofar as we can determine it, the buddha-vacana, first transmitted shortly after the end of Shakyamuni Buddha's life by his main disciples, at first came to consist of two major sets of texts. The first set is known as Sutras, and it is comprised of the discourses of the Buddha (or in some cases of his disciples, but with his sanction), relating the events in his past and present lifetimes and his practical and philosophical teachings. The second set, known as the Vinaya, presents the ethical discipline and monastic rules that regulate the life of the *sangha,* or community, as they were laid down by the Buddha. Collectively, these two sets form the core of what is known as Dharma, or Buddhist doctrine.

In addition, Buddhist canons include texts that provide further explanation and guidance in the Dharma, such as commentaries on the Sutras and Vinaya, treatises on philosophical topics, and ritual and meditative manuals. Broadly known as Shastra, or exegesis, this type of work derived its authority not from being buddha-vacana, but from being authored by those scholiasts, philosophers, and meditation masters who came to be regarded by later Buddhists as of the highest accomplishments and explicatory skills. Perhaps the most important genre of Shastra texts is the collections known as Abhidharma ("Further Dharma"), which consist of systematic analyses and classifications of doctrine composed by scholastic masters as early as three hundred years after the Buddha.

Despite general agreement among Buddhist traditions on the principle that the words of a Buddha and the further exegeses by great masters of philosophy and meditation are what constitute authority and canonicity, there has also been profound disagreement among these traditions about conceptions of what a Buddha is and what a Buddha teaches, and in turn about which masters best explicated the most efficacious and reliable means to liberation. In addition to such sectarian differences, various regional and linguistic divisions have contributed to the compilation of a number of separate canons. Thus, in speaking of the major sources of Buddhism that will inform these volumes, it is necessary to briefly identify the religion's major sectarian and regional divisions.

The Buddhist world today can be divided according to three major traditions, each of which traces its origins to developments in India, presently inhabits a more or less definable geographic region outside India, and subscribes to a distinctive body of scriptural sources, which the followers regard as the most authentic version of the Dharma. The Theravada ("Teaching of the Elders") tradition was the first of the three historically to form a distinct community (fourth century C.E.), and today it continues to thrive in the countries of Sri Lanka, Thailand, Myanmar (Burma), Laos, and Cambodia. The Theravada corpus of scripture—known as the Tripitaka ("Three Baskets") because of its division into the three sections of Sutra, Vinaya, and Abhidharma, described above—was rendered into written form in the Pali language by Sri Lankan elders in the first century B.C.E., but its origins are traced back to a council convened shortly after the end of the Buddha's life in the early fifth century B.C.E., during which his leading disciples orally recited the Buddha's words and began committing them to memory. Theravadins regard their texts as conserving the Dharma as it was originally taught and practiced by Shakyamuni and his most accomplished followers, who are known as *arhats,* or "worthy ones." Their Tripitaka establishes fundamental Buddhist teachings on the nature of suffering, the selflessness of persons, the impermanence of all phenomena, and the path of nonviolent ethics and meditation, which leads to liberating wisdom.

The second major Buddhist tradition, which has called itself the Mahayana ("Great Vehicle") because it has seen its teachings as superior to those of the Theravada and the other (now defunct) preceding early Indian schools, developed in the first centuries of the common era in North India and Central Asia, and has long since come to be the predominant form of Buddhism followed in the East Asian countries of China, Korea, Vietnam, and Japan. While the content of the Vinaya and Abhidharma portions of its canon is closely modeled (with notable exceptions) on texts from the earlier Indian schools (which Mahayanists have labeled collectively as Hinayana, or "Small Vehicle"), the Mahayana also presented a new, divergent scriptural dispensation in its Sutra literature. Composed originally in Sanskrit, these Mahayana Sutras were said to be a higher form of buddha-vacana, which had been kept from the inferior Hinayana Buddhists, until the capabilities of humans had evolved enough to employ this more difficult, but also more efficacious, Dharma. Popular texts such as the *Perfection of Wisdom, Lotus, Teaching of Vimalakirti, Flower Garland, Descent into Lanka,* and *Pure Land* Sutras promoted a new spiritual ideal, the career of the paragon figure of compassion and insight, the *bodhisattva* ("enlightenment being"). Focusing on the philosophical and practical tenets espoused in these newly emergent Sutras, the great Indian masters of the first millennium of the common era composed explicatory treatises that would come to stand as centerpieces in the Mahayana canons. Most important are the works of the Madhyamika, or "Middle Way," school, which expounded on the central idea of *shunyata*, or "emptiness," and those of the Yogacara ("Yoga Practice") school, which developed influential theories on the mind and its construction of objective realities. The subsequent history of Mahayana as it was transformed in East Asia is a complex and varied one, but in the long run two practically oriented schools, namely the Pure Land and Meditation (commonly known in the West by its Japanese name, Zen) schools, emerged as the most popular and remain so today. These schools supplement their canons with texts containing the discourses and dialogues of their respective patriarchs.

The third Buddhist tradition to appear on the historical scene, beginning around the sixth century c.e., is the Vajrayana ("Thunderbolt Vehicle"), commonly known as Tantric Buddhism. The Vajrayana survives today in the greater Tibetan cultural areas of Asia, including the Himalayan kingdoms of Sikkim, Nepal, and Bhutan. Tantric Buddhists regard themselves as Mahayanists, and include in their canon all of the major Mahayana texts mentioned above. However, the Vajrayana itself also claimed a new and divergent dispensation of the Buddha's word, in the form of texts called Tantras. While not philosophically innovative, the Tantras offered novel systems of meditative disciplines and ritual practices known as *sadhanas*. Followers of the Vajrayana maintain that the Tantras are the highest and final words of the Buddha, esoterically preserved until the circumstances were right for their exposure to humanity. As the name Vajrayana suggests, the uniqueness of the Tantras lies in their claim to be providing the most powerful and expeditious means of attaining enlightenment. Like their East Asian Mahayana counterparts, Tantric Buddhists also reserve a place of eminence in their canons for the compositions of their most accomplished masters, who are known as *mahasiddhas,* or "great adepts."

HINDUISM

What we in the twentieth century call Hinduism is in fact a set of religious practices that have developed over three thousand years of Indian history and have a great variety of textual sources. That history begins with the four Vedas—oral compositions of people who called themselves Aryans and who were the ancestors of many of the inhabitants of India today. The term Veda means "knowledge," and these four works comprise the accompaniment to Vedic sacrifice—the main form of worship for the early Aryans. Sacrifice usually involved an animal or vegetable offering to one of the many Vedic gods. The first Veda, the *Rig Veda*, is the oldest (c. 1500 B.C.E.), and comprises the mythological hymns of the sacrifice. The second, the *Yajur Veda*, contains directions on how to conduct the ritual; the third, the *Sama Veda*, contains accompanying musical chants. The final Veda, the *Atharva Veda*, includes hymns for fertility, healing, and other everyday uses in the domestic context, apart from the public sacrifice.

The second set of works important to Hinduism is more philosophical in nature. These works are the Upanishads (c. 900–300 B.C.E.), and consist of speculation about the power behind the sacrifice, called *brahman*, and the nature of the sacrificing self, called *atman*. The Upanishads also contain the beginnings of a system of belief in reincarnation—more properly called the transmigration of the individual self—through the endless cycle of births, deaths, and sufferings, called *samsara*. The Upanishadic philosophers believed that the key to liberation from this cycle of suffering was the union between the atman and brahman. Around 200 B.C.E., these initial ideas were developed into an elaborate science of meditation called Yoga, by the philosopher Patanjali. His treatise, the *Yoga Sutras*, inaugurated the system of yoga as we know and practice it today.

While the Vedas, Upanishads, and *Yoga Sutras* reflect the religious practices of the upper strata, or castes, of Indian society, there was very little textual evidence for popular religious practices until the emergence of the epics, the *Mahabharata* and the *Ramayana*. The *Mahabharata* is the story of the tragic war between cousins, the Kauravas and the Pandavas. The *Ramayana* depicts the exploits of Rama—a hero said to be the *avatar*, or manifestation, of the god Vishnu. In rescuing his wife Sita from the demon Ravana, Rama slays Ravana and rids the world of the evil. Many see these two epics as the source of popular theology prevalent in India today. They are the first texts that make extensive mention of the classical Hindu pantheon—Shiva, Vishnu, Brahma, and Devi, or the goddess. The *Mahabharata* is also the source of the *Bhagavad Gita*—the *Song to the Lord Krishna*, who, in human form, acts as a charioteer in the war. Particularly in the nineteenth and twentieth centuries, the *Bhagavad Gita* has inspired much popular devotion as a Hindu response to the Christian missionary movement.

Near the end of the period of the composition of the epics (c. 200 C.E.), many kings, especially in North India, began to patronize these popular deities and build temples to house them. Such temples had texts called Puranas attached to them; the term *purana* literally means "story of the olden times." Puranas are encyclopedic compilations that praised the exploits of particular deities—Vishnu, Shiva, Brahma, and the Devi, mentioned above. Notoriously difficult to date, the Puranas range from 200 C.E. to 1700 C.E. Another important set of texts, called Dharma Shastras, emerged at about this period; these were elaborate law books that codified daily life according to rules concerned with purity and pollution. The most famous of these is the *Manavadharmashastra*, or the *Laws of Manu*. The Puranas and the Dharma Shastras provide the bulk of the material upon which the modern Hindu tradition draws, and they originate in all regions of India.

The wide geographical spread of the Puranas is partly due to the fact that devotional movements were not exclusive to the northern Gangetic plain, where the Vedas and Upanishads were composed, but were inspired equally by the South Indian, or Dravidian, civilizations. These devotional movements were called *bhakti,* literally meaning "belonging to." A *bhakta* is someone who "belongs to" a particular god, and has chosen that god for devotion. Beginning in the eighth century C.E., the South Indian bhaktas wrote poetry that became an influential source for Hinduism. The collection of poems by the Tamil saint Nammalvar, the *Tiruvaymoli*, has attained the same canonical status as the Vedas, and is called the Tamil Veda. In addition, the Bengali saint Caitanya inspired a bhakti movement devoted to Krishna in the late fifteenth century C.E.; his followers wrote treatises, among them the *Haribhaktirasamrta-sindhu* and *Haribhaktivilasa,* that explain the theology and ritual of devotion to Krishna. Many northern and western Indian poets, such as Mirabai (born c. 1420 C.E.) and Tukaram (1608–1649 C.E.), have contributed significantly to the huge corpus of bhakti poetry and theology that Hindus read and recite today.

The final major source for the study of Hinduism is the Vedanta philosophical tradition, whose development and systematization is attributed to the teacher Shankara in the ninth century C.E. Shankara, and his major successor, Ramanuja (twelfth century C.E.), developed their philosophy through commentaries, called *bhasyas,* on the two main texts of Vedanta—the *Vedanta Sutras* and the *Brahma Sutras.* These texts summarize the doctrine of the Upanishads, mentioned above. In his classic work, *Brahmasutrabhasya,* Shankara argues a philosophy of nonduality (*advaita*). For him, the perceptions of the mind and the senses are simply *avidya*, ignorance. In ignorance, we perceive a duality between subject and object, self and the source of self. This perception of duality prevents the self (atman) from complete identity with brahman. When complete identity is achieved, however, there is liberation of the self from all ignorance.

These manifold sources—the Vedas, the Upanishads, the epics, the Puranas, the Dharma Shastras, the diverse corpus of bhakti poetry, and Vedanta philosophy—make up the spiritual foundations of Hindu practice today.

NOTES

1. HINDUISM

1. John Hick, *Evil and the God of Love* (London, 1968), 5.
2. *Bṛhadāranyaka Upaniṣad* 3.2.12; 4.4.5, in *The Thirteen Principal Upanishads,* 2d ed., trans. Robert Ernest Hume (London: Oxford University Press, 1931; reprint 1975). All subsequent citations from the Upanishads are taken from this translation.
3. *Manusmṛti* 12.3–9, in *The Laws of Manu,* trans. Wendy Doniger with Brian K. Smith (London: Penguin Books, 1991), 278–79. All subsequent quotations from this text are taken from this translation.
4. *Bhagavad Gītā* 3.35, from *The Bhagavad-gītā: Krishna's Counsel in Time of War,* trans. Barbara Stoler Miller (New York: Bantam Books, 1986). All subsequent quotations from this text are taken from this translation.
5. *Tiruccatakam* by Māṇikkavāchakar, 90, in *Sources of Indian Tradition,* vol. 1, ed. Ainslie T. Embree (New York: Columbia University Press, 1988), 347.
6. From the *Bhāgavata Purāṇa* 10.6.1–20; 30–44, in *Hindu Myths: A Sourcebook Translated from the Sanskrit,* trans. Wendy Doniger O'Flaherty (Harmondsworth, Middlesex, England: Penguin Books, 1975), 214–17.
7. In *Sources of Indian Tradition,* ed. Embree, 350.
8. *Cittaviśuddhiprakaraṇa,* 24–38, in *Sources of Indian Tradition,* ed. Embree, 195, 196. This passage is taken from a text produced by a Buddhist Tantric sect, but the sentiments expressed aptly convey the position of Hindu Tantric ideology as well.
9. Wendy O'Flaherty, *The Origins of Evil in Hindu Mythology* (Berkeley and Los Angeles: University of California Press, 1976), 58.
10. *Viṣṇudharma Purāṇa,* ch. 25, cited in Rajendra Chandra Hazra, *Studies in the Upapurāṇas, I: Saura and Vaiṣṇava Upapurāṇas* (Calcutta: Calcutta Sanskrit College Research Series, vol. 11, 1958), 128.

11. O'Flaherty, *Origins of Evil,* 65.
12. *Bhūridatta Jātaka,* no. 543, verses 153c–156, in O'Flaherty, *Origins of Evil,* 5.
13. *Jaiminīya Brāhmaṇa* 1.98–99, in O'Flaherty, *Origins of Evil,* 249.
14. *Viṣṇu Purāṇa* 1.6.14–15; 29–31. Cited in O'Flaherty, *Origins of Evil,* 48.
15. *Bhāgavata Purāṇa* 1.3.24; 2.7.37; 11.4.22; 10.40.22; in O'Flaherty, *Origins of Evil,* 188.
16. David R. Kinsley, *The Sword and the Flute: Kālī and Kṛṣṇa—Dark Visions of the Terrible and the Sublime in Hindu Mythology* (Berkeley: University of California Press, 1975), 139, 144–45.
17. *Viṣṇu Purāṇa* 1.5.1–18, in O'Flaherty, *Origins of Evil,* 51.
18. *Mahābhārata* 3.181.11–20, in O'Flaherty, *Origins of Evil,* 23.
19. *Skanda Purāṇa* 1.20.40.173–85, in O'Flaherty, *Origins of Evil,* 23.
20. *Vāyu Purāṇa* 1.8.77, in O'Flaherty, *Origins of Evil,* 24.
21. *Liṅga Purāṇa* 1.40.72–83, in O'Flaherty, *Origins of Evil,* 40.
22. Max Weber, *The Sociology of Religion,* trans. Ephraim Fischoff, 4th ed. (London: Methuen, 1963), 145.

2.BUDDHISM

1. See "Literary Sources of World Religions" in *God,* Pilgrim Library of World Religions, ed. Jacob Neusner (Cleveland: The Pilgrim Press, 1997), xxvi.
2. Mahaniddesa 304.
3. From the *Pañca Rakṣā Kathāsāra,* trans. Todd T. Lewis, in Lewis, "The Power of Mantra: A Story of the Five Protectors," *Religions of India in Practice,* ed. Donald S. Lopez Jr. (Princeton, N.J.: Princeton University Press, 1995), 229–30.
4. See "Literary Sources of World Religions" in *God,* xxvii.
5. Nichiren, quoted in Richard Causton, *The Buddha in Daily Life* (London: Rider, 1995), 126; translation slightly modified.
6. *Scripture of the Lotus Blossom of the Fine Dharma,* trans. from the Chinese by Leon Hurvitz (New York: Columbia University Press, 1976), 58.
7. From Karen Lang, "Aradeva and Candrakirti on Self and Selfishness," in *Buddhism in Practice,* ed. Donald Lopez (Princeton, N.J.: Princeton University Press, 1995), 387.

8. Bhavaviveka, *Tarkajvala,* in *To See the Buddha,* trans. Malcolm David Eckel (San Francisco: HarperCollins, 1992), 175–76.

9. *Once the Buddha Was a Monkey: Aryasura's Jatakamala,* trans. from the Sanskrit by Peter Khoroche (Chicago: University of Chicago Press, 1989), 6–7.

10. Bhavaviveka, *Tarkajvala,* 176.

11. *Dhammapada,* v. 279.

12. Eugene W. Burlingame, *Buddhist Legends* (Cambridge: Harvard University Press, 1921), vol. II, 258–59; translation modified.

13. *Majjhimanikaya* 87, trans. Thanissaro Bhikkhu, in Bhikkhu, *The Mind like Fire Unbound* (Barre, Mass.: Dhamma Dana Publications, 1993), 49.

14. *Samyuttanikaya* V. 420.

15. Buddhaghosa, *The Path of Purification,* trans. Nanamoli (Kandy, Sri Lanka: Buddhist Publication Society, 1975), 569.

16. See "Literary Sources of the World Religions" in *God,* xxvii; *God,* 71.

17. *Land of Bliss,* introductions and English translations by Luis Gómez (Honolulu: University of Hawaii Press, 1996), 199.

18. *Selections from Buddhist Literature,* ed. Clarence H. Hamilton (Indianapolis: Bobbs-Merrill, 1952), 125.

19. Yoshifumi Ueda and Dennis Hirota, *Shinran: An Introduction to His Thought* (Kyoto: Hongwanji International Center, 1989), 303.

20. See Charles Hallisey and Anne Hansen, "Narrative, Sub-ethics, and the Moral Life: Some Evidence from Theravada Buddhism," *Journal of Religious Ethics* 24 (1996): 319–21; the research among the Khmer refugees was done by Anne Hansen.

21. This paragraph depends on Hallisey and Hansen, "Narrative, Sub-ethics, and the Moral Life," 319–21.

22. Zenkei Shibayama, *Zen Comments on the Mumonkan* (New York: Harper & Row, 1974), 289.

23. Dharmasena Thera, *Jewels of the Doctrine,* trans. Ranjini Obeyesekere (Albany: State University of New York Press, 1991), 224.

24. *The Three Worlds according to King Ruang: A Thai Buddhist Cosmology,* trans. Frank Reynolds and Mani Reynolds (Berkeley, Calif.: Berkeley Buddhist Studies Series, 1982), 243.

25. From Kamalashila, *Bhavanakrama,* trans. Stephen Beyer, in *The*

Experience of Buddhism, ed. John Strong (Belmont, Calif.: Wadsworth, 1995), 159–60.

26. Buddhaghosa, *Visuddhimagga,* trans. Nanamoli, 340.

27. *The Dhammapada,* trans. John Ross Carter and Mahinda Pali-hawadana (New York: Oxford University Press, 1987), v. 127.

28. *Letters of Nichiren,* trans. Burton Watson et al., ed. Philip Yampolsky (New York: Columbia University Press, 1996), 58–59.

29. *The Dhammapada,* v. 1.

30. *Selections from Buddhist Literature,* ed. Clarence H. Hamilton (Indianapolis: Bobbs-Merriill, 1952), 29.

31. That is, the five physical senses plus the mind.

32. *Samyuttanikaya* 2:18–21, in *The Experience of Buddhism,* trans. and ed. John Strong, 100–101.

33. Sallie King, "Awakening Stories of Zen Buddhist Women," in *Buddhism in Practice,* ed. Donald Lopez (Princeton, N.J.: Princeton University Press, 1995), 517, 518, 521.

3.CHRISTIANITY

1. See *Sacred Texts and Authority,* Pilgrim Library of World Religions (Cleveland: The Pilgrim Press, 1998).

2. See Marcus Aurelius, *Meditations,* trans. Maxwell Staniforth (London: Penguin, 1964). Staniforth's introduction (pp. 7–17) is excellent.

3. See J. M. Rist, *Stoic Philosophy* (Cambridge: Cambridge University Press, 1969), especially the chapter titled "Suicide," 233–55. Staniforth, p. 166, represents the opinion that the statement about the Christians originated as a marginal note which was later incorporated into the text.

4. See Tacitus, *Annals* 15.37–44. The passage is cited in full in Bruce Chilton and Jacob Neusner, *Trading Places Sourcebook: Readings in the Intersecting Histories of Judaism and Christianity* (Cleveland: The Pilgrim Press, 1997), 182–87.

5. That story is told in Bruce Chilton and Jacob Neusner, *Trading Places: The Intersecting Histories of Judaism and Christianity* (Cleveland: The Pilgrim Press, 1996), 37–58.

6. See Eusebius, *The History of the Church from Christ to Constantine,* trans. G. A. Williamson (Baltimore: Penguin, 1967), 2.25.

7. For the emphatic wording of the prayer of Jesus, and its Aramaic original, see Bruce Chilton, *Jesus' Prayer and Jesus' Eucharist: His Personal Practice of Spirituality* (Valley Forge, Pa.: Trinity Press International, 1997), 36–38.

8. In fact, Jesus' own eschatology included two further dimensions. His definition of the kingdom provided for a distinctive view of what made for the purity acceptable to God and for an emphasis on the outward, inclusive range of the dominion. See Bruce Chilton, *Pure Kingdom: Jesus' Vision of God,* Studying the Historical Jesus 1 (Grand Rapids, Mich.: Eerdmans, 1996). Those dimensions are not included here because they did not amount to distinctive types of eschatology within the formative periods of Christianity. Still, emphasis on the purity and on the outward extension of God's dominion are characteristic of Christianity in most periods.

9. For the examples and their elucidation, we are indebted to John M. Dillon, "Looking on the Light: Some Remarks on the Imagery of Light in the First Chapter of the *Peri Archon,*" *The Golden Chain: Studies in the Development of Platonism and Christianity* (Aldershot, U.K.: Variorum, 1990), 215–30 (essay XXII).

10. This is Dillon's main point (see p. 225), and his citation of *On First Principles* 1.1.6 demonstrates it admirably.

11. See *Trading Places,* 203–9.

12. For a useful discussion, see C. Breytenbach and P. L. Day, "Satan," *Dictionary of Deities and Demons in the Bible,* ed. K. van der Toorn, B. Becking, and P. W. van der Horst (Leiden: Brill, 1995), 1369–80.

13. H. Crouzel, "Origen and Origenism," *New Catholic Encyclopedia* (New York: McGraw-Hill, 1967), 767–74.

14. For an accessible discussion of the relevant texts, see G. W. Butterworth, *Origen on First Principles* (New York: Harper & Row, 1966), 57, 251. There is a splendid note on the subject in Henry Chadwick, *Early Christian Thought and the Classical Tradition* (New York: Oxford University Press, 1966), 158 n. 15.

4.JUDAISM

1. For an extended discussion of this matter, see Jacob Neusner, *The Theology of the Oral Torah: Revealing the Justice of God* (Kingston and Montreal: McGill-Queens University Press, 1998). This chapter further follows the compelling argument and analysis of David Kraemer in *Responses to Suffering in Classical Rabbinic Literature* (New York: Oxford University Press, 1995).
2. We take up the Messiah theme in the setting of the afterlife in a later volume in this series.
3. Kraemer, *Responses to Suffering,* 22 ff.
4. Treating suffering apart from death and life after death, as in the present setting, separates what in Judaism are not to be treated in isolation, since suffering and death form the tickets of admission to the Garden of Eden/the world to come/the resurrection of the dead and the like. Judaism deals with evil and suffering only in the grand scheme of salvation and redemption.
5. Kraemer, *Responses to Suffering,* 111.

5.ISLAM

1. A. J. Arberry, *The Koran Interpreted* (New York: Macmillan, 1955).
2. Ibid.
3. 'Abd al-Malik b. Hishām, *Sīrat al-Nabī,* 4 vols. (Cairo: Dār al-Turāth, n.d.).
4. Modified from A. J. Wensinck, *The Muslim Creed* (Cambridge: University Press, 1932), 191.
5. Arberry, *The Koran Interpreted.*
6. Ibid.
7. Ibid.
8. Ibid.
9. Al-Ghazzālī, *Iḥyā' 'ulūm al-dīn,* 5 vols. (Beirut: Dār al-Fikr, 1991).
10. Qāḍī 'Iyāḍ b. Mūsā, *Tartīb al-madārik,* 3 vols., ed. Ahmed Bekir (Beirut: Dār Maktabat al-Ḥayāh, 1967).
11. Ibid.
12. Fazlur Rahman, *Major Themes of the Qur'ān* (Minneapolis: Bibliotheca Islamica, 1989; 2d printing), 127–28.

13. Arberry, *The Koran Interpreted.*
14. Wensinck, *The Muslim Creed,* 126.
15. Ibid., 191.

LITERARY SOURCES OF THE WORLD RELIGIONS

1. A. J. Arberry, *The Koran Interpreted* (New York: Macmillan, 1955).
2. For example, a version of the Chinese Buddhist canon, published in Tokyo in the 1920s, is made up of 55 Western-style volumes totaling 2,148 texts!